Like No Other: The Life of Christ
Bible Studies for Life: Small Group Member Book

© 2014 LifeWay Press®

ISBN: 9781430035015

Item: 005680983

Dewey Decimal Classification Number: 232.9

Subject Heading: JESUS CHRIST \ CHRISTIANITY \ CHRISTIAN LIFE

Eric Geiger
Vice President, Church Resources

Ronnie Floyd
General Editor

David Francis
Managing Editor

Gena Rogers
Sam O'Neal
Content Editors

Philip Nation
Director, Adult Ministry Publishing

Faith Whatley
Director, Adult Ministry

Send questions/comments to: Content Editor, *Bible Studies for Life: Adults*, One LifeWay Plaza, Nashville, TN 37234-0175; or make comments on the Web at *www.BibleStudiesforLife.com.*

Printed in the United States of America

For ordering or inquiries, visit *www.lifeway.com*; write LifeWay Small Groups; One LifeWay Plaza; Nashville, TN 37234-0152; or call toll free (800) 458-2772.

All Scripture quotations, unless otherwise indicated, are taken from the Holman Christian Standard Bible®, copyright 1999, 2000, 2002, 2003, 2009 by Holman Bible Publishers. Used by permission.

Bible Studies for Life: Adults often lists websites that may be helpful to our readers. Our staff verifies each site's usefulness and appropriateness prior to publication. However, website content changes quickly so we encourage you to approach all websites with caution. Make sure sites are still appropriate before sharing them with students, friends, and family.

Social Media

 Connect with a community of *Bible Studies for Life* users. Post responses to questions, share teaching ideas, and link to great blog content. ***Facebook.com/BibleStudiesForLife***

 Get instant updates about new articles, giveaways, and more. **@BibleMeetsLife**

The App

Simple and straightforward, this elegantly designed app gives you all the content of the Small Group Member Book—plus a whole lot more—right at your fingertips. Available in the iTunes App Store and for Android devices; search "**Bible Studies for Life.**"

Blog

At ***BibleStudiesForLife.com/blog*** you will find magazine articles and music downloads from LifeWay Worship. Plus, leaders and group members alike will benefit from the blog posts written for people in every life stage—singles, parents, boomers, and senior adults—as well as media clips, connections between our study topics, current events, and much more.

Training

 For helps on how to use Bible Studies for Life, tips on how to better lead groups, or additional ideas for leading this session, visit: ***www.ministrygrid.com/web/biblestudiesforlife.***

His name is Jesus. He is like no other.

He never wrote a book. Yet more books have been written about Him than about any other individual in all of history.

He never wrote a song. But more songs have been composed and sung about Him than about anyone else in the world.

He never traveled more than 300 miles from His home. Yet you can find only a few places in the entire world where people have not heard His name.

Jesus.

To simply worship or acknowledge Jesus as a great person, great prophet, or great leader is to insult Him. He is far more than all of these. He is God who become a man; He is God in the flesh. In Him, the perfect wedding of Deity and humanity coexist, yet are not mixed.

Jesus became like us in order to bring us back into a relationship with God. He entered our world in order to give us a way out of it. He died so that we may live. He gives us life for now and life for eternity.

This study is for all of us. Jesus Christ is more than theology on a shelf, a picture of a man with a halo, or miracles from long ago. He is your friend like no other.

Tony Evans

Dr. Evans is founder and senior pastor of Oak Cliff Bible Fellowship in Dallas, TX, founder and president of the Urban Alternative, and chaplain of the NBA's Dallas Mavericks. He is the author of several books and studies, including *The Power of God's Names*. For more information, visit *TonyEvans.org*.

contents

4   *Session 1: Promised Like No Other*

14   *Session 2: A Birth Like No Other*

24   *Session 3: Power Like No Other*

34   *Session 4: Teachings Like No Other*

44   *Session 5: A Death Like No Other*

52   *Session 6: Resurrected Like No Other*

62   *Session 7: Ascended Like No Other*

72   *Session 8: Exalted Like No Other*

82   Leader Guide

SESSION 1

PROMISED LIKE NO OTHER

How do you decide whether someone is believable?

QUESTION *#1*

#BSFLpromised

LIKE NO

Jesus is the promised Messiah.

THE BIBLE MEETS LIFE

Two brothers ran into the house and saw a bowl full of eggs their mom was about to boil. The older brother said, "I'll give you a dollar if you let me break three of these on your head." "Promise?" the younger one asked. "Of course," the older one answered.

Soon, the first egg dripped down the younger brother's face. Then the second. He didn't care; he had his heart set on the promise of the dollar. But as the boy stood there waiting for the third egg, his older brother darted off laughing. "I'm not breaking the third one," the older brother called back, "because that would cost me a dollar!"

Life often serves up broken promises. People disappoint us. Leaders mislead us. And over time, trust cracks like an egg spilling its contents over us. So, how do we know Jesus is who He claimed to be? Why should we believe Him? We know this and we believe Him because He was promised through indisputable prophecy that ultimately came to pass. Let's begin our study of the life of Jesus by going back to a promise that is like no other.

WHAT DOES THE BIBLE SAY?

Isaiah 53:2-12 *(HCSB)*

2 He grew up before Him like a young plant and like a root out of dry ground. He didn't have an impressive form or majesty that we should look at Him, no appearance that we should desire Him. **3** He was despised and rejected by men, a man of suffering who knew what sickness was. He was like someone people turned away from; He was despised, and we didn't value Him. **4** Yet He Himself bore our sicknesses, and He carried our pains; but we in turn regarded Him stricken, struck down by God, and afflicted. **5** But He was pierced because of our transgressions, crushed because of our iniquities; punishment for our peace was on Him, and we are healed by His wounds. **6** We all went astray like sheep; we all have turned to our own way; and the LORD has punished Him for the iniquity of us all. **7** He was oppressed and afflicted, yet He did not open His mouth. Like a lamb led to the slaughter and like a sheep silent before her shearers, He did not open His mouth. **8** He was taken away because of oppression and judgment; and who considered His fate? For He was cut off from the land of the living; He was struck because of my people's rebellion. **9** They made His grave with the wicked and with a rich man at His death, although He had done no violence and had not spoken deceitfully. **10** Yet the LORD was pleased to crush Him severely. When You make Him a restitution offering, He will see His seed, He will prolong His days, and by His hand, the LORD's pleasure will be accomplished. **11** He will see it out of His anguish, and He will be satisfied with His knowledge. My righteous Servant will justify many, and He will carry their iniquities. **12** Therefore I will give Him the many as a portion, and He will receive the mighty as spoil, because He submitted Himself to death, and was counted among the rebels; yet He bore the sin of many and interceded for the rebels.

His seed (v. 10)—The Hebrew word refers either to what was sown to produce crops or to a person's offspring or descendants. In Isaiah 53:10, the phrase "His seed" likely indicated the Messiah's spiritual descendants—people who would enter His family of faith through commitment to Him.

Portion (v. 12)—The Hebrew word refers either to a share of the spoils of victory in war or to a parcel of land allotted to or possessed by people. The Messiah would be victorious, and He would be rewarded for His faithfulness to God's redemptive purpose.

> **What surprises you about this description of Christ?**

Isaiah 53:2-3

A pastor walked with a soap manufacturer down the streets of New York. Noticing all the advertisements, stores, and clothing promoting a life of ungodliness, the soap manufacturer remarked to the pastor: "The gospel you preach hasn't done much good. There's a lot of filth in this world."

The two men walked a few more blocks before they encountered a homeless man covered in grime. "The soap you sell hasn't done much good," the pastor reflected. "There's a lot of filth in this world."

The soap manufacturer chuckled and said: "Ah, but you're wrong. Soap is only useful when it is applied."

"Exactly," said the pastor. "And so it is with the gospel."

A lot of people misunderstand what Jesus came to give us—and how He came to give it. When they look at the life of Jesus, they see things they'd rather not see: pain, rejection, endurance, obscurity, and humility. You see, Jesus didn't come as a pop star or as a reality-TV king. Isaiah 53:2-3 shows us He had no stately form or majesty. He wasn't handsome. Instead, He was despised. He knew grief and hung out with sorrow. The promise God gave was that our Savior would be rejected by His own people.

We see in the Gospels how this promise came true:

▶ "He came to His own, and His own people did not receive Him" (John 1:11).

▶ "Then they all cried out together, 'Take this man away!'" (Luke 23:18).

Have you ever felt rejection? It cuts deep. It knocks the wind out of you. It's a pain that lingers, causing you to doubt your own worth. So when it happens, you might try to ignore it. People often try to eat, shop, or entertain their way out of it.

But Jesus didn't run from rejection. He knew God always has a purpose for the pain. And because of that truth, He willingly embraced it. The gospel message is that Jesus endured rejection so that we can have abundant life. But His sacrifice must be applied in order for that life to take effect.

"I PROMISE!"

What makes a promise believable for you? Rank the following factors according to their level of importance when it comes to evaluating the promises of other people. (Give a 1 to the most-important factor and a 5 to the least-important.)

____ The content of the promise itself.

____ The trustworthiness of the person giving the promise.

____ Your desire for the promise to be true.

____ Your past experiences with people and promises.

____ The consequences of the promise falling through.

Which of these factors contribute to your evaluation of the promises in God's Word?

"Our Lord came down from life to suffer death.
The Bread came down to hunger.
The Way came down on the way to weariness.
The Fount came down to thirst."

—ST. AUGUSTINE OF HIPPO

Isaiah 53:4-9

The Bible has been substantiated both historically and archeologically as more accurate than any other book handed down through time. Research and analysis by historians, linguists, sociologists, and archeologists have demonstrated the soundness of the Scriptures through forensic science, the discovery and study of ancient literature, and much more.

The Bible is set apart from all other books in one other way: its prophetic accuracy. A classic example is the foretelling of Jesus' birth in Bethlehem. In Micah 5:2, the prophet Micah told of our Savior's birth more than 700 years before it happened. Matthew recorded the fulfillment of this prophecy in Matthew 2:1-6. What makes this prophecy stand out is the obscurity of Bethlehem. Had Micah mentioned a major metropolis in Israel, people could say he had merely guessed well. Yet Micah recorded the mind of God by pinpointing this remote region as the site of Christ's birth.

Micah's prophecy is just one of several hundred that have already been fulfilled in Scripture. God knows the beginning from the end, and prophecy involves the recording of His thoughts before an event historically happens.

Isaiah 53 also contains a number of prophecies, including Jesus' piercing, His scourging, and even His silence in the face of oppression. The passage also mentions that our own iniquities would be placed on Jesus as our sinless Savior: "He Himself bore our sicknesses, and He carried our pains" (v. 4). Jesus came not only to bear our sins, but also our burdens.

In your pain, know this one truth: you are not alone. Jesus sees. He knows. He cares. He's been there. And because He has suffered, He offers a comfort not merely rooted in intellectual assent, but in compassionate understanding.

> *Which prophecies about Jesus in these verses do you find compelling?*
>
> QUESTION #3

> *How can you testify to Christ bearing your sickness and carrying your pain?*
>
> QUESTION #4

Isaiah 53:10-12

Have you ever reached that place where your best contacts, connections, relationships, and everywhere else you had previously put your hope just wasn't enough? We sometimes call that "hitting rock bottom." It's at that moment we realize how much we need Jesus. What other people offer in those moments comes up lacking, yet it's in those times we experience Jesus' presence all the more.

After all, Isaiah prophesied that Jesus would come so that He could help us. The crushing and the anguish He went through justified us before God. As He bore our sin, we also read that he "interceded for the rebels" (v. 12). What's more, now that our sin has been atoned for, His intercession has not ceased. In fact, because of His sacrifice, Jesus now intercedes from a position of strength (see Romans 8:34).

Through His death, Jesus secured our pardon. Through His resurrection, He secured our daily hope. **He is the promised Messiah who not only came for us but also remains as our lifeline and assurance.**

You can take comfort in the authenticity of Scripture; it's been confirmed by history, archeology, and the sheer number of fulfilled prophecies. Therefore, turning to Jesus as your help is the wisest thing you could ever do. He is uniquely positioned to provide guidance, comfort, strength, and power. Jesus' life and ministry were like no other. And the prophecies that point to Him are like no other. Jesus is that "friend who stays closer than a brother" (Prov. 18:24). He is "a helper who is always found in times of trouble" (Ps. 46:1). He is your Mediator and your Master. He is your risen King.

When have you felt like only Jesus was enough?

QUESTION **#5**

LIVE IT OUT

How can the fulfillment of these promises and prophecies help strengthen your faith? Consider taking one of these steps this week:

▶ **Discover God's promises.** As you read the Bible, highlight any verses that contain a promise from God.

▶ **Trust His plan.** Make it a point to actively proclaim your trust in God each day. When you pray, acknowledge His plan for your life and declare your intention to trust Him.

▶ **Search His prophecies.** Use a Bible dictionary or concordance to look up Old Testament prophecies about Jesus. Consider how each prophecy underscores the truth of who Jesus is.

God keeps His promises. He is dependable and faithful. He sent Jesus as the Messiah—just as He said He would. God will prove Himself trustworthy to you if you will seek Him.

It's All About Jesus

At the start of 2012, I managed to stumble across a number of read-through-the-Bible plans that caught my attention. One of those plans was to read the entire Bible in 90 days. I thought: Whoa! The idea seemed daunting, but also intriguing, so I decided to tackle the plan.

To continue reading "It's All About Jesus" from *ThreadsMedia.com*, visit *www.BibleStudiesforLife.com/articles.*

My group's prayer requests

....
....
....
....
....
....
....
....
....
....

My thoughts

SESSION 2

A BIRTH LIKE NO OTHER

How do you typically introduce yourself to someone new?

QUESTION #1

Jesus is fully human and fully God.

THE BIBLE MEETS LIFE

He could have been born in a castle, seeing as He came as King. Yet the babe in the barn arrived with little worldly notice to parents both unknown and poor. No flowers. No nursemaid. Not even the animals took much notice as they nestled in for the night.

Heaven's heart had beat in the womb of a woman for the previous nine months—if you could call her a woman. History records her as a young teen, yet full of a faith greater than the years she had known. Out of her came omnipotence now cloaked in limitation. She nursed spirit clothed in skin.

Her child was flesh, bones, sinew, and blood. Yet He was also the perfection of the divine. He felt hunger because He was fully human, yet He would later feed 5,000 because He was fully God. He grew thirsty because He was fully human, yet He would one day walk on water because He was fully God.

His was a birth like no other—like nothing else in history—for in Him God was robed with humanity.

WHAT DOES THE BIBLE SAY?

Luke 1:26-35 *(HCSB)*

26 In the sixth month, the angel Gabriel was sent by God to a town in Galilee called Nazareth,

27 to a virgin engaged to a man named Joseph, of the house of David. The virgin's name was Mary.

28 And the angel came to her and said, "Rejoice, favored woman! The Lord is with you."

29 But she was deeply troubled by this statement, wondering what kind of greeting this could be.

30 Then the angel told her:

Do not be afraid, Mary, for you have found favor with God.

31 Now listen: You will conceive and give birth to a son, and you will call His name Jesus.

32 He will be great and will be called the Son of the Most High, and the Lord God will give Him the throne of His father David.

33 He will reign over the house of Jacob forever, and His kingdom will have no end.

34 Mary asked the angel, "How can this be, since I have not been intimate with a man?"

35 The angel replied to her: "The Holy Spirit will come upon you, and the power of the Most High will overshadow you. Therefore, the holy One to be born will be called the Son of God.

Favored woman (v. 28)—God's grace or favor is His goodness in action. God blessed Mary by giving her a major role in His redemptive purpose.

Deeply troubled (v. 29)—The Greek verb from which this term is derived means "to be stirred up, unsettled, agitated, or confused." It was used to describe water being agitated or stirred up.

Overshadow (v. 35)—The angel used the term to express God's exercising His creative energy ("the power of the Most High") to cause Mary to conceive. No sexual overtones are present. The emphasis is on God's power to create.

Luke 1:26-31

If anyone knew about the impossibility surrounding a virgin birth, it was Luke, the writer of this Gospel. A physician by trade and a Greek by culture, Luke's mind was committed to details, data, and order. His writings reflect organization and careful research. No hint of fairy tale, myth, or fable surrounds his words.

Yet it was precisely a doctor who wrote about the virgin birth. Twice in this passage, Luke used the word "virgin." Twice he drew attention to the single detail that's critical to everything else. In other words, Luke's emphasis highlighted God's role in this event. This was no ordinary conception. Without it, Mary's child would have been like everyone else's. In this one unique conception and birth, the immaterial and the material merged. Nobility entered poverty while Divine holiness combined with humanity.

> *Since Jesus existed before time, why is it significant that He came as a baby?*
>
> QUESTION #2

Matthew also highlighted the virgin birth: "Jacob fathered Joseph the husband of Mary, who gave birth to Jesus who is called the Messiah" (Matt. 1:16). In the original Greek language, these verses tell us that Joseph was Mary's husband, but he wasn't Jesus' father. Jesus was conceived by the Holy Spirit so that He would have a divine nature, and His divinity made it possible for Jesus to be sinless. His humanity had both a heavenly origin through the power of God's Spirit and an earthly origin through the virgin named Mary.

The angel Gabriel was sent by God to communicate the unique circumstances of Jesus' conception and birth to Mary. Being visited by a supernatural being had to be frightening, not to mention hearing such incredible news. But Gabriel reminded Mary not to be afraid because, "The Lord is with you."

Mary's situation was unique, but she was under God's direction and favor—and that's a good place to be.

Luke 1:32-33

As a pastor, I get to perform my fair share of weddings. One of my favorite experiences is praying with the bride and her bridesmaids before the ceremony. After the wedding comes the reception, which is a party where people gather together with plenty of good food and festive music to congratulate the newlyweds and celebrate their union. Weddings are wonderful.

As followers of Jesus Christ, we're all going to attend a special wedding one day. When the marriage of the Lamb comes, Christ's bride will be ready. We, the church, will wear wedding garments that are called "the righteous acts of the saints" (Rev. 19:8). The marriage supper of Jesus Christ (see Rev. 19:6-7) will be a real celebration, too, because Jesus wasn't born simply to take away the sins of the world—although that surely is more than enough to celebrate by itself! Jesus was also born to reign as Messiah and King forever. Isaiah told us that the Messiah's kingdom is one that will never end (see Isa. 9:7).

Gabriel made Mary aware of the unique role Jesus would play in history—and for all eternity. Jesus reigns now in history, and He will also reign in the ultimate glory of eternity.

Jesus has already established the rules of His reign. He has set the tone through His life. In His kingdom, neither race nor gender nor wealth nor social status determines our place with Him (see Gal. 3:28). Instead, Christ gives strength to those who look to Him for strength. Forgiveness trumps bitterness, and the amount of money you have doesn't matter. What matters is the heart.

The baby born of the virgin came not only to live and to die, but to reign. Through Jesus, God has set up a kingdom that will never be destroyed nor abandoned. His kingdom and reign will last forever.

> **What are the differences between living in a democracy and living under Jesus as the Sovereign Ruler?**

QUESTION #3

Luke 1:34-35

Isaiah told us about our most wonderful gift when he wrote that "a child will be born to us, a son will be given" (Isa. 9:6).

Given. Notice how carefully the Holy Spirit chose to word this prophecy. The son is "given" to us. As the Son of God, Jesus already existed—He wasn't coming into existence for the first time. Yet the child was "born" of a virgin because God supernaturally brought about Jesus' human birth as a result of divine conception in human flesh.

The two natures of Jesus Christ form what theologians call the "hypostatic union." That's a big term, but it simply means that Jesus is made up of undiminished Deity and perfect humanity. He became no less God when He became human. **Jesus was not 50 percent human and 50 percent God; rather, Mary gave birth to the God-man who was both fully God and fully man at the same time.**

Jesus was born of God so that He might be "God with us"—which is the meaning of His name, Immanuel. We read in Colossians 1:19 that "God was pleased to have all His fullness dwell in Him."

The Bible often equates Jesus with God, reinforcing this relationship. Genesis 1:1 tells us that God created the world, and Colossians 1:16 tells us that all things were created by Christ Jesus. The God of Genesis 1:1 is also the God of Colossians 1:16. Jesus Christ is distinct from God the Father in His Person, yet equal with God in His Deity. He took on human flesh in order to be born as a baby in a world full of darkness. He came for the purpose of making the invisible God visible to us in history.

Jesus' birth was a birth like no other because He is Deity like no other. Jesus came to earth as the Son of God so that we may know God and experience Him more fully.

> *Since Jesus lived as a man, why is it important to understand He is God?*

QUESTION #4

> *Jesus is fully God and fully man. How does that truth influence your choices this week?*

QUESTION #5

DOUBLE ENCOURAGEMENT

The fact that Jesus is both fully human and fully divine offers us two pieces of great news. Use the spaces below to record what you find encouraging about Jesus' human nature and His divine nature.

JESUS' HUMANITY

JESUS' DIVINITY

"Nothing in fiction is so fantastic as this truth of the Incarnation."

—J. I. PACKER

LIVE IT OUT

How do you respond to the truth that Jesus is fully human and fully God? Consider taking one of the following steps:

▶ **Dig deeper.** Ask your pastor to recommend a book, article, or podcast that can help you better understand Jesus' nature.

▶ **Get to know God's Word.** Meditate on Jesus' divinity and humanity by memorizing Hebrews 4:15-16 over the next few days. Concentrate on the truths those verses express.

▶ **Invite someone to know Jesus.** Pray for an opportunity to talk with someone who may not realize Jesus is both fully human and fully God. Be honest and encouraging as you share the truth of God's Word.

You have a friend who sticks closer than a brother. That friend is your Savior. He is your friend because He is fully human. He is your Savior because He is fully God.

Mary: All We Know

I don't want to appear negative, but let us begin by admitting what we do not know about Mary. We know nothing of her parents, birth, or youth. We do not know her age when Jesus was born, what thoughts she may have had about Him as her Son grew into manhood. And, we do not know for certain when, where, and how she died. Having said all of this, exploring what the New Testament does tell us about her is still worthwhile. After all, Mary is the most noteworthy female in the entire New Testament.

To continue reading "Mary: All We Know" from *Biblical Illustrator* magazine, visit *BibleStudiesforLife.com/articles*.

My group's prayer requests

_____

_____

_____

_____

_____

_____

_____

_____

_____

_____

My thoughts

SESSION 3

POWER LIKE NO OTHER

What forms of power really get your attention?

QUESTION #1

Jesus has power over all my fears.

THE BIBLE MEETS LIFE

We can expect bad days, weeks, and even months. They come with living on a fallen earth with fallen humanity as a fallen child of the King. But we're never to define peace by our circumstances. That's because we have a far better source for peace—and for courage. In fact, it's the only true Source.

Jesus told us clearly: "I have told you these things so that in Me you may have peace. You will have suffering in this world. Be courageous! I have conquered the world" (John 16:33).

We all face uneasy times. Whether economic, health-related, relational, or financial, these situations often cause us to feel powerless or overwhelmed. But as we'll see in this study, Jesus has power like no other. And He will use His power on our behalf.

To see what I mean, let's look at an event in Jesus' ministry where He revealed His power on behalf of His followers.

WHAT DOES THE BIBLE SAY?

Mark 4:35-41 *(HCSB)*

35 On that day, when evening had come, He told them, "Let's cross over to the other side of the sea."

36 So they left the crowd and took Him along since He was already in the boat. And other boats were with Him.

37 A fierce windstorm arose, and the waves were breaking over the boat, so that the boat was already being swamped.

38 But He was in the stern, sleeping on the cushion. So they woke Him up and said to Him, "Teacher! Don't you care that we're going to die?"

39 He got up, rebuked the wind, and said to the sea, "Silence! Be still!" The wind ceased, and there was a great calm.

40 Then He said to them, "Why are you fearful? Do you still have no faith?"

41 And they were terrified and asked one another, "Who then is this? Even the wind and the sea obey Him!"

The other side (v. 35)—Refers to the eastern bank of the Sea of Galilee, which at the time was territory belonging to the Gentiles.

Sleeping (v. 38)—This is the only instance recorded in the Gospels in which Jesus was specifically identified as being asleep.

Mark 4:35-38a

On Sundays, I preach two one-hour messages each week. I also typically have meetings with different church leaders. Needless to say, I'm worn out by the time Sunday afternoon comes along. When I get home, I head straight for my favorite chair to rest. Before I know it, I'm asleep.

Jesus wasn't reclining in an easy chair in Mark 4. It was night. It was dark. It was windy. The boat was rocking fiercely in the middle of a savage storm that threatened to sink it. How do you fall asleep during that? Granted, Jesus was surely exhausted after a long day of teaching and ministry, but He did more than just nod off. When Jesus went to sleep on that boat, He did so on purpose.

How do I know this? Verse 38 says He was "sleeping on the cushion." Jesus had grabbed a pillow and moved to the back of the boat. When you're stretched out and asleep on a pillow, you mean to be that way.

But how could Jesus sleep through such a squall when His disciples feared for their lives? Perhaps He wanted to see if they would trust what He said more than the circumstances around them. Jesus had already told them what they were going to do. He said, "Let's cross over to the other side of the sea." He planned to reach the far shore safe and sound, and no storm would alter His plan.

Jesus' disciples did what we often do when we listen to a sermon or participate in a Bible study—they heard the message without applying the meaning. They heard the words but missed the promise. When you find yourself in a problem, don't forget the promise. Remember what Jesus said. He's right there with you, so trust Him to calm the waves.

> **In what ways do we typically respond to frightening situations?**
>
> QUESTION #2

Mark 4:38b-39

The location of the Sea of Galilee in the Jordan Rift causes tempests to flare up violently with little or no notice. In the deepest dark of night, out in the middle of the sea, the storm surely must have caught the disciples off-guard. The storm tested not only their boating expertise, but also their emotions.

Sometimes it doesn't seem like God is in tune with our situations. When we find ourselves in stormy conditions—health, financial, relational, or job troubles—we may want to say: "Jesus, please wake up! We're in a mess, and we're afraid."

It is precisely in those times when we feel so weak and helpless that Jesus' power is most visibly strong. **God does some of His best work in those moments we don't think He's working at all.**

▶ Sometimes God lets you hit rock bottom so that you will discover He is the Rock at the bottom.

▶ Sometimes God allows you to get into a situation only He can fix so that you will see Him fix it.

Whatever the case, you can trust His work is motivated by His heart of love for you (see Rom. 8:28).

Jesus got up from His slumber and spoke to the sea, "Silence! Be still!" Two brief commands, and the storm obeyed. The word for "silence" literally means "hold your peace." Jesus told the storm to be quiet. To stop its noise. To hush its fuss. Similar to a parent correcting an unruly toddler, Jesus told the sea to settle down—and it did.

Thunder and lightning might be chasing each other all around you. The wind may be blowing unexpected and unpleasant circumstances into your life. Nothing looks right. Nothing looks promising. But it's precisely in those times that Jesus' power trumps the storm.

> *How have you learned that God really does care about His people?*
>
> QUESTION #3

> *How can we reconcile the truth of Jesus' power with the fact that He doesn't always calm the storm?*
>
> QUESTION #4

Mark 4:40-41

The story is told of a flight that hit some unusual turbulence, tossing the airplane side to side in strong gusts of wind. Lightning hit nearby. No one felt safe—no one except for one small child. He sat preoccupied with his notebook and pen. To look at him, you never would have guessed he was on a plane in the middle of a storm. A passenger nearby asked the young boy, "Aren't you afraid?"

He just looked up from his paper for a moment, smiled, and said: "Nah. My dad is the pilot."

When you know who's in the cockpit, even turbulence can be OK. Because when life seems out of control, it's simply out of *your* control. Knowing Who sits at the control panel ought to usher in a heart of peace.

Peace means different things to different people, but the peace Jesus offers is like no other. His peace produces internal calm in the midst of external chaos. We experience the peace of Christ when we trade in our fears of the storm for a healthy fear and reverence of Him—when we shift our gaze from the sea to the Savior.

Paul told us to respond to God's peace the same way the storm responded to Jesus that night on the Sea of Galilee. "And let the peace of the Messiah ... control your hearts" (Col. 3:15). The Greek word used for "control" means "to umpire." In baseball, an umpire declares the way things are. Whatever he says should happen is what happens. Likewise, whatever Jesus says about a matter, that's what it is. It's settled. So when He says "Be courageous! I have conquered the world" (John 16:33), that's all we need to hear. And we should respond accordingly—with courage.

Your world may be falling apart, but you don't have to fall apart with it. Responding to Jesus' presence and power in your life allows you to let go of your fear and replace it with peace—His peace. That doesn't mean you won't have problems, but it does mean your problems won't have you. You can rest comfortably on your cushion, because He's got it under control.

> *In your everyday life, what does it mean to respond to Jesus' power?*

QUESTION #5

ALL MY FEARS

Which of these images connects with your deeper fears?

How can you more fully incorporate Jesus into your methods for handling your fears?

"He is no fool who gives what he cannot keep in order to gain what he cannot lose."

—JIM ELLIOT

LIVE IT OUT

In what ways can you let go of your fears as you trust in Jesus' power? Consider the following suggestions:

▶ **Write it down.** Make a list of the most pressing external problems that give rise to your internal fears. Pray over this list in connection with the truth found in John 16:33.

▶ **Watch your words.** Each day, assess whether your speech is more focused on your problems or on Jesus, who is the solution. Seek to speak more openly about Jesus.

▶ **Pray together.** Consider ways you can encourage others to trust Christ. Look for evidence of people struggling with turmoil and invite them to pray with you for peace.

You really don't know how much faith you have until your faith gets tested. Keep your eyes on Jesus in the midst of life's storms, ask for His help, and trust Him to get you to the other side.

A Father's Call to Fight

A Father's Call to Fight

Each year when summer rolls around, my wife and kids honor me on Father's Day. For me, Father's Day is not only a day to reflect on the greatest blessings God's given me — my family — but also a day to reflect on God, the ultimate Father.

To continue reading "A Father's Call to Fight" from *ParentLife* magazine, visit *BibleStudiesforLife.com/articles*.

My group's prayer requests

....

....

....

....

....

....

....

....

....

....

My thoughts

SESSION 4

TEACHINGS LIKE NO OTHER

What makes your favorite teacher your favorite teacher?

QUESTION **#1**

LIKE NO

Jesus teaches us how to live and calls us to follow Him.

THE BIBLE MEETS LIFE

Whatever you'd like to learn, someone will teach it to you. Whether you're hoping to play the piano, plant a garden, program a computer, or anything else—you can find people to help you on your way. The best teachers instruct, lead, correct, guide, and encourage. And with their help, you gain a new skill set.

But where do you go to learn how to live well? Where do you go when you want to know how to be a better person or overcome challenges? Who do you seek to teach you what's best or how to make right choices?

Will you find those answers in magazines? Talk-shows? YouTube?

Jesus Christ is the greatest resource you can find to teach you about life. He's not simply a religious icon or a distant God speaking in ethereal or intangible terms. His teaching is clear and gets to the heart of what it means to live life to the fullest. Let's consider how the Giver of life is also the Teacher of life.

WHAT DOES THE BIBLE SAY?

Mark 1:21-22; 10:17-22 *(HCSB)*

1:21 Then they went into Capernaum, and right away He entered the synagogue on the Sabbath and began to teach.

22 They were astonished at His teaching because, unlike the scribes, He was teaching them as one having authority.

10:17 As He was setting out on a journey, a man ran up, knelt down before Him, and asked Him, "Good Teacher, what must I do to inherit eternal life?"

18 "Why do you call Me good?" Jesus asked him. "No one is good but One—God.

19 You know the commandments: Do not murder; do not commit adultery; do not steal; do not bear false witness; do not defraud; honor your father and mother."

20 He said to Him, "Teacher, I have kept all these from my youth."

21 Then, looking at him, Jesus loved him and said to him, "You lack one thing: Go, sell all you have and give to the poor, and you will have treasure in heaven. Then come, follow Me."

22 But he was stunned at this demand, and he went away grieving, because he had many possessions.

Capernaum (1:21)—A city located on the northwestern shore of the Sea of Galilee. Jesus used this city as His main base of operations throughout His public ministry.

Commandments (10:19)—Jesus' list is from the second half of the Ten Commandments, which focused on behavior and relationships with other people.

Mark 1:21-22

We don't know what Jesus specifically taught in this passage, but one thing is clear: those who heard Him teach knew He did so with authority. "They were astonished at His teaching because, unlike the scribes, He was teaching them as one having authority."

For the rest of us, any authority we have is limited to the roles we've been given. Whether you're the President of the United States or a mother corralling a 3-year-old, your authority only extends so far. Yet Christ's authority is unlimited because it rests intrinsically within Him. He taught with authority like no other because He *is* that authority. He embodies absolute truth. He said, "I am the way, the truth, and the life" (John 14:6).

Jesus backed up His authority with His actions. He demonstrated the dependability of His words with miracles:

▶ He paid his taxes with a coin out of the mouth of a fish (see Matt. 17:24-27).

▶ He cast out demons His disciples could not (see Mark 1:23-27).

▶ He raised the dead (see Mark 5:35-42).

▶ He turned a few fish and bread into a giant meal for thousands (see Mark 6:30-44).

▶ He walked on water His followers feared (see Mark 6:45-52).

If Jesus' teachings had gone no further than the people who originally heard Him speak, His authority might have gotten lost on the dusty shelves of history. But that's not what happened. In fact, shortly before He returned to His Father, Jesus commanded His followers to go out in the world and teach on His behalf. Out of His authority, He gave us this charge (see Matt. 28:18-20).

Jesus sits in a position of authority today, and He has called us to both live and teach His words from a position of authority as well (see Eph. 2:6).

What's the difference between knowledge and authority?

QUESTION #2

ASSESSMENT: JESUS' TEACHING

Information

How confident do you feel in your understanding of biblical doctrine?

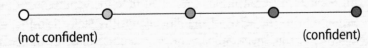

(not confident)　　　　　　　　　　　　　　　　(confident)

Application

How confident do you feel in your ability to do what Jesus wants you to do?

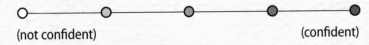

(not confident)　　　　　　　　　　　　　　　　(confident)

Communication

How confident do you feel in your ability to teach others about Jesus and how to follow Him?

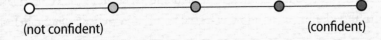

(not confident)　　　　　　　　　　　　　　　　(confident)

As a group, how can we help one another become more comfortable with understanding and applying Jesus' teachings?

Mark 10:17-21a

John 11:35 is the shortest verse in the Bible. You probably know it by heart: "Jesus wept." The verse only has two words, but they reveal an abyss of emotion. They don't tell us Jesus teared up. They don't say He dabbed the corners of His eyes with His holy hand towel. Instead, those two words let us know precisely that Jesus did more than just cry—He wept. Not only that, but He wept in front of others.

Yet why should we be surprised? Time after time the Scriptures record our Savior experiencing great emotion and love. The Jesus of the Bible is not the stoic, halo-topped, European actor we so often watched on biblical movies growing up. He's not a flannel-board Messiah of one-dimension. Our Lord felt great compassion, and that compassion motivated His actions in love. We read:

▶ "When He saw the crowds, He felt compassion for them" (Matt. 9:36).

▶ "As He stepped ashore, He saw a huge crowd, felt compassion for them, and healed their sick" (Matt. 14:14).

▶ "Moved with compassion, Jesus reached out His hand" (Mark 1:41).

▶ "When the Lord saw her, He had compassion on her" (Luke 7:13).

▶ "As He approached and saw the city, He wept over it" (Luke 19:41).

In Mark 10, Jesus met a young man who wanted to experience something more out of life. This man wanted someone to teach him about eternity, and so he came to Jesus.

Out of His love, Jesus affirmed this man's actions and gave him one very powerful invitation: sell all he had and give it to the poor. Because in doing so, he would store up treasures in heaven. Out of His love, Jesus urged this man to let go of all the things that were keeping him from experiencing true treasure.

> *How does Jesus' approach help us love those we disagree with?*
>
> QUESTION #3

Mark 10:21b-22

What the young man in this story learned—and what we need to learn—is that Jesus' teaching calls for a response. To merely admire Jesus as a great Teacher without applying the truths He taught is to forfeit the treasure of which He spoke. It's the same as declaring you really don't believe Him after all. **Obedience to what Jesus teaches is proof that you believe Him.**

Acting in belief on Christ's words requires faith. And faith is measured by your life, not your lips. It involves your feet, not just your feelings. In fact, to not live by faith is to call God a liar. It's to challenge His integrity because faith means you are taking Him at His word. In other words, faith is acting like something *is* so even when it's not so in order that it might be so simply because God said so.

Yet faith is only as powerful as the object to which it is attached. You could have all the faith in the world that your car was suddenly going to sprout wings and fly you to the moon, but you would still end up on the ground. Yet when you attach your faith to Jesus Christ and His Word—and you respond by obeying what He has revealed—that's the kind of faith that moves mountains (see Matt. 17:20). Responding to Jesus' teaching means trusting Him enough to do what He says.

Jesus is the world's greatest Authority on how to live life to the fullest. And He has given us His teaching in His Word. To read it, study it, discuss it, and yet not apply it makes no sense at all. Therefore, choose to listen to Jesus' teaching and respond with trustful obedience.

> *Why is it loving for Jesus to call us to do something difficult or even painful?*
>
> QUESTION #4

> *How have Jesus' teachings changed the way you live?*
>
> QUESTION #5

LIVE IT OUT

How can you apply Jesus' teaching to your daily life? Consider the following suggestions this week:

▶ **Read.** Read through one of the Gospels this week. As you come across Jesus' different teachings, reflect on how living by that teaching would benefit your life.

▶ **Commit.** As you read God's Word, make a conscious, deliberate decision to obey what it teaches. Pray through that commitment for the rest of the day.

▶ **Teach.** Consider leading a Bible study or teaching a class for kids, students, or adults. Let God use you to communicate the teachings of Jesus to others.

As a disciple of Jesus Christ, you have a daily opportunity to sit at the feet of Jesus. You can learn from Him—and learn how to experience life to the fullest. Take advantage of that blessing today.

Gray Areas

We live in a world of infinite possibilities, even when we're addressing important moral and ethical issues. For some questions, there seems to be no right or wrong answers. What's worse, in other situations, there seems to be several right answers. Not only do good people disagree, really good people really disagree.

To continue reading "Gray Areas" from *HomeLife* magazine, visit *BibleStudiesforLife.com/articles.*

My group's prayer requests

_____
_____
_____
_____
_____
_____
_____
_____
_____

My thoughts

SESSION 5

A DEATH LIKE NO OTHER

Why do we care when famous people pass away?

Jesus' death is the heart of the gospel.

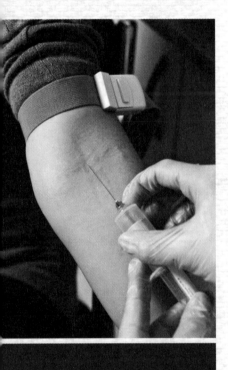

THE BIBLE MEETS LIFE

"Would you give your blood to help save your sister?" the doctor asked Timothy, looking into the young boy's eyes. Timothy's sister was suffering from an illness he had survived. And because they shared a rare blood type, Timothy was the ideal donor.

The boy hesitated after the doctor's question. His chin began to quiver as he fought back tears. Then, with a solemn strength and even the hint of a smile, he said, "Yes. I'll do it."

An hour later, Timothy watched the blood flow out of his arm and into a plastic tube. Quiet for most of the procedure, he finally asked, "Doctor, when will I die?" The boy thought donating his blood meant giving *all* his blood. Timothy had willingly offered the greatest sacrifice out of love for his sister.

Let's explore a death like no other—the day when Jesus, the One through whom all things were created, willingly gave Himself up out of His great love for us.

WHAT DOES THE BIBLE SAY?

Matthew 27:28-31,45-50,54 *(HCSB)*

28 They stripped Him and dressed Him in a scarlet military robe.

29 They twisted together a crown of thorns, put it on His head, and placed a reed in His right hand. And they knelt down before Him and mocked Him: "Hail, King of the Jews!"

30 Then they spit on Him, took the reed, and kept hitting Him on the head.

31 When they had mocked Him, they stripped Him of the robe, put His clothes on Him, and led Him away to crucify Him.

45 From noon until three in the afternoon darkness came over the whole land.

46 About three in the afternoon Jesus cried out with a loud voice, "Elí, Elí, lemá sabachtháni?" that is, "My God, My God, why have You forsaken Me?"

47 When some of those standing there heard this, they said, "He's calling for Elijah!"

48 Immediately one of them ran and got a sponge, filled it with sour wine, fixed it on a reed, and offered Him a drink.

49 But the rest said, "Let's see if Elijah comes to save Him!"

50 Jesus shouted again with a loud voice and gave up His spirit.

54 When the centurion and those with him, who were guarding Jesus, saw the earthquake and the things that had happened, they were terrified and said, "This man really was God's Son!"

Elijah (v. 47)—The prophet Malachi wrote that God would send Elijah before His day of judgment on the earth (see Mal. 4:5). The witnesses mistook Jesus' words as a reference to that prophecy.

> **What do these verses teach us about Jesus?**

QUESTION #2

Matthew 27:28-31

Nobody likes bullies. They push you. Shove you. Mock you. It's bad enough to be bullied by people you don't really know and don't particularly care for. But to be pushed into the path of bullies by people you love and trust—that's a far deeper pain.

Jesus came to bring salvation to His own, yet His own rejected him. The religious leaders handed Jesus over to brutal Roman soldiers who stripped Him, robed Him in purple, stuck a crown of thorns on His head, knelt down before Him, and mocked Him. In their mockery, they stuck a reed in His right hand as if it were a king's scepter. Then they spat on Him. They took that same reed and beat Him with it.

As I read this passage, I keep getting stuck on the word "reed," which was a slender stick or stem. This isn't the first time we see a reed in the Bible. Isaiah wrote about another reed, but it was a bruised reed— something weak and vulnerable—not one used to mock or strike: "He will not break a bruised reed, and He will not put out a smoldering wick; He will faithfully bring justice" (Isa. 42:3).

The bruised reed in Isaiah 42:3 stands for those of us who've been hurt. Bullied. Broken. Bent. The verse speaks of God's faithfulness to those who've been harassed by life's circumstances—or by people we loved and trusted: a hurtful mate. A toxic parent or relative. A backstabbing coworker.

How ironic that the One who came to bring justice to the bruised reeds in this life was bruised Himself by a reed. He who would cup the wilted reed in His hand and nurture it back to health and strength stood bloodied, beaten, and mocked by those He came to save. And yet He said nothing in return.

The soldiers led Him as a sheep to the slaughter even though He was the true King on the cross. Jesus was bullied, but bullies didn't put Him on the cross and nails didn't hold Him there. His love for us held Him there.

Jesus willingly sacrificed His life so that we could be saved.

Matthew 27:45-50

How do we explore the tension between the truth of God's love and the events in these verses?

QUESTION **#3**

When I experience an allergic reaction, my eyes water, my nose itches, and I often sneeze. Many of you know firsthand about allergies. If you're allergic to an animal, you'll usually get away from it as soon as you can.

God is "allergic" to sin in the sense that He will have absolutely nothing to do with it. He is holy. Holiness is the very nature and character of God. And since holiness and sin are diametrically opposed, God and sin cannot hang out together. Furthermore, since sin is a part of who we are, that means God will not hang out with us.

Yet there's still hope. God, out of His great love, created a way for you and me—in spite of our sin—to enter His presence. That way is through the cross. That way has been made possible through Jesus, the sinless sacrifice who bore our sins.

When Jesus hung on the cross, all of the sins of the 7 billion people alive today—as well as those of the billions who came before us—fell upon Him. All the sins, both actions and attitudes, of countless billions of people were hurled upon Jesus Christ.

How bad was that moment?

What emotions have you experienced while discussing Jesus' death?

QUESTION **#4**

We often think the pain of the cross came from the whip that stripped the skin from Jesus' back. Or from the crown of thorns that dug deeply into His skull. Or from the nails in His hands and feet. But all that agony was nothing compared with that moment in time when He looked up to heaven and groaned, "*Elí, Elí, lemá sabachtháni?*" That is, "My God, My God, why have You forsaken Me?"

At that moment, Jesus became sin, severing Himself from the fullness of the intimacy He had always known with His Father. As the sin of the whole world shot through His body, God the Father turned away from His Son.

Matthew 27:54

I used to go to a barber in Dallas who had a sign on his window that read: "In God we trust. Everyone else pays cash." It was his shop, so he could make the rules.

In a similar way, our world is God's "shop"—His kingdom. He makes the rules. And He requires payment through only one source: the death, burial, and resurrection of His Son Jesus Christ. That is the only way to satisfy His holy demand to pay for sin.

The earth itself revolted when the Son of God hung there to die. "The earth quaked and the rocks were split" (Matt. 27:51). Why? Because Jesus had formed and shaped the earth (see John 1:3); therefore, the very earth He created now protested.

Those who stayed with Jesus while He hung on the cross that day became frightened by the earth's response. Who wouldn't have? If you've ever been in a storm, if you've ever seen the blue sky turn green just before the fierce winds of a tornado pass through, if you've ever watched wall hangings first shake and then fall as the ground moves beneath you in an earthquake—you know the fear that can rise up.

At times like these, people get real religious, real fast! At those times, we come face to face with our own humanity and the awesome power of God's hand, and we wake up and realize in just whose world we live. The centurion in this passage had just such an experience. So did the guards keeping watch. Their experience at the death of Jesus led them to only one response: "This man really was God's Son!"

> **When in your own life did you encounter the truth that Jesus is God's Son?**
>
> QUESTION #5

LIVE IT OUT

What does Jesus' death mean for your life? Consider the following options for responding to His sacrifice:

▶ **Confess.** Ask God to forgive you of your sins in light of Jesus' death on the cross.

▶ **Show gratitude.** Set aside time each day to intentionally express gratitude to Jesus for the sacrifice He made on your behalf. Let that gratitude influence your words and actions.

▶ **Invite others.** Invite someone to join you next week as your group discusses what happened after Jesus died on the cross. The focus on Christ's resurrection is a great time to introduce someone to the gospel.

We are all sinners born with a sin nature, but thanks be to God through His Son Jesus Christ. Forgiveness is available. Forgiveness has been paid for. And forgiveness is for you.

My group's prayer requests

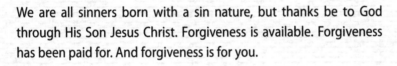

SESSION 6

RESURRECTED LIKE NO OTHER

When were you excited to experience something firsthand?

#BSFLresurrected

QUESTION #1

LIKE NO

Jesus is alive—and we can live forever.

THE BIBLE MEETS LIFE

Nothing is quite the same as seeing something majestic in person. Maybe it was the Grand Canyon, the Statue of Liberty, or the Eiffel Tower. You'd seen photographs, but when you visited in person— wow!—it was a whole different experience. Pictures didn't do it justice.

Similarly, a friend can talk nonstop about how thrilling it is to ski, ride a certain roller coaster, or see a particularly inspiring movie. However, it's a whole different experience when you strap on the skis, step onto the ride, or sit in the darkened theater yourself. We can get caught up in another person's enthusiasm, but it's totally different when the experience is our own.

The most incredible moment in the Bible—no, in all of history— was the moment Jesus came back to life. We can read of those who saw Jesus alive, and we can marvel at the proof of this event, but our knowledge doesn't have to stop there.

Wouldn't it be great to know firsthand that Jesus is alive?

WHAT DOES THE BIBLE SAY?

Matthew 28:1-10 *(HCSB)*

1 After the Sabbath, as the first day of the week was dawning, Mary Magdalene and the other Mary went to view the tomb.

2 Suddenly there was a violent earthquake, because an angel of the Lord descended from heaven and approached the tomb. He rolled back the stone and was sitting on it.

3 His appearance was like lightning, and his robe was as white as snow.

4 The guards were so shaken from fear of him that they became like dead men.

5 But the angel told the women, "Don't be afraid, because I know you are looking for Jesus who was crucified.

6 He is not here! For He has been resurrected, just as He said. Come and see the place where He lay.

7 Then go quickly and tell His disciples, 'He has been raised from the dead. In fact, He is going ahead of you to Galilee; you will see Him there.' Listen, I have told you."

8 So, departing quickly from the tomb with fear and great joy, they ran to tell His disciples the news.

9 Just then Jesus met them and said, "Good morning!" They came up, took hold of His feet, and worshiped Him.

10 Then Jesus told them, "Do not be afraid. Go and tell My brothers to leave for Galilee, and they will see Me there."

The other Mary (v. 1)—Likely refers to the mother of Jesus' lesser-known disciples James and Joseph (see 27:56).

Dead men (v. 4)—The guards did not perish; rather, they lost consciousness and fell to the ground.

Matthew 28:1-7

Why does It matter that Jesus physically rose from the dead?

QUESTION #2

Boxer Joe Louis had a spotless record of 27-0 going into his fight with the German Max Schmeling. Everyone expected Louis to win—but he didn't. Twelve rounds into a fifteen-round bout, Schmeling knocked Louis to the mat. The hero had fallen.

This was not just a fight between men. This was in 1936, when Nazism was at its height and Germany was developing into the picture of evil. The fight had been promoted as a battle between democracy and fascism. Right and wrong. Good versus evil. And it appeared evil had won.

But the story wasn't over. Two years later, a second fight was scheduled between Louis and Schmeling. Louis came out swinging. In just under a minute, Schmeling went down for the third and final time. Louis had won the match with a knockout. The one who was considered the enemy—the one who had once been hailed as the victor—discovered he had lost.[1]

On the Sunday after His crucifixion and death, Jesus Christ did what no one else has ever done: He got up. Jesus Christ delivered death its deciding blow. His resurrection places Him in a class by Himself. He is the risen Lord. And because of that, He is the only One through whom salvation can be granted. After all, you cannot place living faith in a dead savior.

In what ways has Jesus' resurrection impacted history?

QUESTION #3

If the resurrection didn't matter, then the stone would have stayed right where it had been placed. But we see in Matthew 28 that the angel of the Lord rolled the stone away. The angel didn't roll it away so Jesus could get out. Jesus had already risen! No, the angel of the Lord rolled the stone away to show the tomb was empty. God wanted everyone to see that evil had lost its victory because Jesus had defeated the grave.

WORSHIP HIM

When the disciples encountered Jesus after His resurrection, their first impulse was to worship Him. The same should be true of us. Read the beginning of Psalm 95 as an act of worship, then express your own feelings about Jesus in the space provided.

PSALM 95:1-6

1 Come, let us shout joyfully to the LORD,
  shout triumphantly to the rock of our salvation!
2 Let us enter His presence with thanksgiving;
  let us shout triumphantly to Him in song.
3 For the LORD is a great God,
  a great King above all gods.
4 The depths of the earth are in His hand,
  and the mountain peaks are His.
5 The sea is His; He made it.
  His hands formed the dry land.
6 Come, let us worship and bow down;
  let us kneel before the LORD our Maker.

"When we preach the resurrection of Christ,
we are preaching the miracle of love."

—BILLY GRAHAM

Matthew 28:8-10

Not only did the empty tomb point to Jesus' resurrection, but the eyewitnesses did so as well. Verse 8 tells us that after the women encountered the angel who told them Jesus had risen, they "ran to tell His disciples."

The disciples also went on to see the resurrected Jesus, and they had no doubt whatsoever that He was alive. Need evidence of their conviction? Look at their lives.

When Jesus was arrested in the garden, His disciples scattered in fear (see Matt. 26:56). They had boasted of their allegiance to Him—the One they thought was to be their ruler and king (vv. 33-35). When the going got tough, however, they all abandoned Him. They just couldn't see how dying was any way to become a king.

But then came Sunday.

The Sunday Jesus rose from the dead made all the difference in the world. As a matter of fact, it made all the difference *for* the world. Sunday was when the disciples' eyes were opened and they learned death couldn't contain Jesus. Over the next 40 days, Jesus appeared to the disciples and many others, up to 500 people at one time, in various settings (see 1 Cor. 15:5-8). We can be assured of this because history validates this truth with how the disciples lived—and died.

Prior to seeing Jesus Christ alive, His disciples trembled, ran away, and hid. Yet after they witnessed the resurrected Lord and were filled with His Holy Spirit, they boldly followed Him and willingly drank of the cup that was His.

James, one of the two who said he was willing to drink the cup when asked by Jesus (see Mark 10:38-39), was the first of the 12 apostles to die for His belief in the resurrected Jesus. The Jews in power despised men like James who were unrelenting in their claim that Christ had risen from the dead. So King Herod, in an attempt to please the Jews, killed James with a sword (see Acts 12:1-2).

Judas Iscariot, of course, died by his own hand soon after betraying Jesus to the authorities for 30 pieces of silver (see Matt. 27:3-9; Luke 22:1-6). All the other original apostles, except for John, were killed because of their commitment to Jesus. While we have more historical evidence of the martyrdom of some of the apostles than of others, history records in some form or fashion that all died a martyr's death except for John, who was exiled to the island of Patmos. In short, each of the apostles died for teaching and proclaiming Jesus Christ as the resurrected and living Savior.

Now, I understand people even today will go to great lengths for high-minded notions or ideals. But think about it: who would knowingly and willingly die for a lie?

The disciples died for an undeniable truth. They saw Jesus alive after He had been crucified and buried. And because of what they'd seen, they knew death would not be the end for them, either. Jesus had come to give eternal life. That was the confident hope in which they died, and it is the same confident hope in which we are to live today.

Jesus is alive!

Why is worship still the appropriate response to the resurrection?

QUESTION #4

How will Jesus' resurrection impact your life in the days to come?

QUESTION #5

LIVE IT OUT

How should you respond to the hope of Jesus' resurrection? Consider the following suggestions this week:

▶ **Seek peace.** Too many people allow the fear of the future to hold them back. Ask the Holy Spirit to help you embrace the peace that comes with eternal life through Christ.

▶ **Celebrate!** Jesus' resurrection remains the best news anyone can hear. Therefore, make a concerted effort to celebrate that miracle this week. Give yourself permission to feel joy.

▶ **Pay it forward.** Someone told you about the gift of eternal life available in Christ. Do the same for someone else by explaining how they can have a future hope in Christ.

The message of Easter is that you and I have the promise of eternal life. We will live forever and love forever. Such good news should affect what we do each day.

Finding Hope in Life's Saturdays

The Bible gives us many of the difficult details concerning the death of Jesus. From His hands and feet being nailed to the cross, to the soldiers gambling over His clothes. We're told in the Gospel of Matthew that "darkness fell across the whole land." That was the first day, a dark day for many reasons. His followers were crushed. They had seen the glory for a while and now it was gone. Hope was lying in a tomb.

To continue reading "Finding Hope in Life's Saturdays" from *Mature Living* magazine, visit *BibleStudiesforLife.com/articles*.

My group's prayer requests

....

....

....

....

....

....

....

....

....

My thoughts

1. Nigel Collins, "Louis-Schmeling: More than a fight," ESPN [cited 15 August 2014]. Available from the Internet: *http://espn.go.com*.

SESSION 7

ASCENDED LIKE NO OTHER

Whose words always catch your attention?

#BSFLascended

LIKE NO

Jesus ascended to heaven but did not leave us alone.

THE BIBLE MEETS LIFE

Want to know what's important to people? Find out what's on their mind when they come to the end of their life. Look at these famous last words, for example:

▶ "I have offended God and mankind because my work did not reach the quality it should have"—Leonardo da Vinci (1519).[1]

▶ "I have tried so hard to do the right"—Grover Cleveland (1908).[2]

▶ "I believe that a life lived for music is an existence spent wonderfully, and this is what I have dedicated my life to"—Luciano Pavarotti (2007).[3]

After His resurrection and just before His ascension, Jesus told His disciples, and us, what mattered to Him. "You will receive power when the Holy Spirit has come on you, and you will be My witnesses" (Acts 1:8). Jesus returned to heaven, but He knew we could not accomplish His mission on our own. We would need the presence and the power of His Spirit to carry out that great work.

WHAT DOES THE BIBLE SAY?

Acts 1:3-11 (HCSB)

3 After He had suffered, He also presented Himself alive to them by many convincing proofs, appearing to them during 40 days and speaking about the kingdom of God.

4 While He was together with them, He commanded them not to leave Jerusalem, but to wait for the Father's promise. "This," He said, "is what you heard from Me;

5 for John baptized with water, but you will be baptized with the Holy Spirit not many days from now."

6 So when they had come together, they asked Him, "Lord, are You restoring the kingdom to Israel at this time?"

7 He said to them, "It is not for you to know times or periods that the Father has set by His own authority.

8 But you will receive power when the Holy Spirit has come on you, and you will be My witnesses in Jerusalem, in all Judea and Samaria, and to the ends of the earth."

9 After He had said this, He was taken up as they were watching, and a cloud took Him out of their sight.

10 While He was going, they were gazing into heaven, and suddenly two men in white clothes stood by them.

11 They said, "Men of Galilee, why do you stand looking up into heaven? This Jesus, who has been taken from you into heaven, will come in the same way that you have seen Him going into heaven."

The Father's promise

(v. 4)—Refers to the gift of the Holy Spirit Jesus had promised His disciples during the Last Supper (see John 16:5-15). This promise was fulfilled on the Day of Pentecost (see Acts 2:1-13).

Acts 1:3

I've spent more than 12 years of my life in biblical education. I chose that path because I had a passion for ministry and God's Word. Despite the depth of my passion, though, an interesting thing happened over time. As I studied God's Word more and more, it seemed that my hunger for it diminished. Reading and studying God's Word became information rather than illumination.

That all changed when I left the classroom and starting using the Bible in ministry. God's Word comes alive as we minister. Sitting face to face with person after person, counseling each one through difficult situations forces me to know what the Lord taught about those circumstances. Preaching in front of thousands of people several times a week—many of whom live in trying circumstances—motivates me to dig deep into the Scriptures and discover all I can to help them. My focus has moved from verbs and tenses to meaning and application.

As we look at Acts 1, remember that the disciples had been with Jesus for three years of solid training. They saw Him perform miracles and heard Him teach. Yet, when we look at the disciples' words and actions during Jesus' trial, it would appear they never heard or saw much that made a difference to them. They doubted. Wandered. Feared. And ran.

Thankfully, everything changed after their Friend and Savior rose from the dead. For 40 days, Jesus spoke to them and gave them a crash course in the kingdom of God. I suspect the disciples absorbed more in those 40 days than in their previous three years with Jesus. Suddenly, Jesus had their undivided attention.

I know the disciples listened closely, now. Jesus' words at this point became very dear to them. What Jesus taught His disciples before His ascension mattered to them. The life and words of Jesus had become the passion of their lives.

The same should be true of us, as well.

> *If you had a limited time with Jesus, what would you most want to learn?*

QUESTION **#2**

PLUGGED IN?

The Holy Spirit is the main source of power for the Christian life.
What helps you "plug in" to that power source in the following areas of life?

At Home

At Work

At Play

Acts 1:4-8

During His last supper with the disciples before His arrest, Jesus said: "It is for your benefit that I go away, because if I don't go away the Counselor will not come to you. If I go, I will send Him to you" (John 16:7). Here in Acts 1, Jesus again promised the presence of His Holy Spirit.

When Jesus was on earth, His actions were constrained by His humanity. Neither His Deity nor His essence was diminished, yet He worked in only one location at a time. When people needed Jesus, they had to meet Him face to face. Things are different with the Holy Spirit because He lives within each follower of Jesus Christ; He goes with us wherever we go. He is always present in full power within each of us—all at the same time. The Holy Spirit is not subject to the limitations of human flesh to which Jesus voluntarily surrendered.

The Holy Spirit is God, a part of the Trinity. The Holy Spirit indwells, transforms, and empowers each believer to live the victorious kingdom life. **The Spirit provides power for you to function as you align yourself under the lordship of Jesus Christ.**

Imagine purchasing a new refrigerator. You excitedly fill the shelves with food and beverages, but the next morning you discover that everything has gone bad. Frustrated, you call the company to complain. After you explain what happened, the technician asks a question that freezes you with embarrassment: "Did you plug it in?"

Jesus has secured for us everything we need to live the empowered life. And the Holy Spirit is the Power Source. His presence provides the power to turn fear into faith, worry into peace, and heartache into hope. He is our source and ever-present help in times of trouble.

> *In your own words, how would you describe the presence and work of the Holy Spirit?*

QUESTION #3

Acts 1:9-11

Notice the verbs Luke used in verses 9-11 to describe Jesus' ascension into heaven.

▶ "He was taken up."

▶ "A cloud took Him out of their sight."

▶ "He was going."

In other words, Jesus' ascension was both visible and physical. This was neither a mirage nor a figment of anyone's imagination. It was a tangible, physical event. In the same way Jesus was resurrected bodily, He ascended bodily.

It's important to realize Jesus physically ascended—not just as a spirit—and He will also physically return. As the disciples watched Jesus ascend, two angels told them, "This Jesus, who has been taken from you into heaven, will come in the same way that you have seen Him going into heaven" (Acts 1:11). No one else has ever ascended from this earth the way Jesus did, and no one is coming back the way He is coming back. He is like no other. He is the distinct and unique message of all creation.

A day is coming when we will experience a real transformation. This incredible change will occur when Jesus Christ returns for His followers, and we are with Him forever.

Why is it important that Jesus' disciples witnessed His ascension?

QUESTION **#4**

How does the promise of Jesus' return influence your daily decisions?

QUESTION **#5**

"Christianity is not one ideology over against other ideologies. It is a life inspired by the Holy Spirit."

—PAUL TOURNIER

LIVE IT OUT

How can we respond in light of Jesus' ascension and eventual return? Consider the following options:

▶ **Plug in.** Begin each day by asking the Holy Spirit to make Himself known in your life. Pray that He will offer clear directions as you weigh options and make decisions.

▶ **Research.** Look through articles, sermons, podcasts, or books in order to broaden your understanding of the Holy Spirit and His role in your life.

▶ **Let go.** Our future is in heaven with Jesus. Therefore, choose to let go of something—a possession, a grudge, a way of life—that keeps you tethered to this world.

You don't know what your last words in this life will be. No one does. However, you can know here and now that you're never alone. God Himself—His Holy Spirit—lives in you!

Afloat and Alone

I don't spend a lot of time on boats, but whenever I find myself on the water, I'm always a little amazed at the power of the current. It's one of those forces that's always there, no matter how still and pristine a body of water might seem, still churning and moving below the surface. Imagine with me that you're on a boat on one of those clear, warm, early summer days. The clouds are few, and the wind is even less, so you cruise out to the middle of the lake on what seems like a sheet of glass.

To continue reading "Afloat and Alone" from *HomeLife* magazine, visit *BibleStudiesforLife.com/articles*.

My group's prayer requests

....

....

....

....

....

....

....

....

....

My thoughts

1. Charles Nicholl, *Leonardo da Vinci: Flights of the Mind* (New York: Penguin Books, 2005).

2. H.P. Jeffers, *An Honest President: The Life and Presidencies of Grover Cleveland* (New York: HarperCollins, 2002).

3. "The last words of Luciano Pavarotti," The Phrase Finder [cited 8 October 2014]. Available from the Internet: *http://www. phrases.org.uk.*

SESSION 8

EXALTED LIKE NO OTHER

What's your favorite way to honor others?

#BSFLexalted

Honor Jesus as Lord.

THE BIBLE MEETS LIFE

I love movies—good movies, at least. But sometimes after the credits roll I find myself wondering, *What happened next?*

As an example, the classic book and movie *Gone With the Wind* ends with this statement: "After all, tomorrow is another day." People used to ask the author, Margaret Mitchell: "What happened when tomorrow came? What happened to Scarlett O'Hara?" Mitchell never had an answer. She had no plans for a sequel, and as far as she was concerned, the story was over.

Jesus' earthly life ended with a great climax: His resurrection, post-resurrection appearances, and a physical ascent to heaven. But have you ever wondered what happened next? To put it another way: What is Jesus up to these days?

The story continues! Jesus is exalted to heaven, and the Book of Ephesians gives us a glimpse into His role and reign right now in our lives. As we look at Ephesians 1 and explore the exalted state of Jesus, we'll see how we are to live in response to Him.

WHAT DOES THE BIBLE SAY?

Ephesians 1:7-10,18-23 *(HCSB)*

7 We have redemption in Him through His blood, the forgiveness of our trespasses, according to the riches of His grace

8 that He lavished on us with all wisdom and understanding.

9 He made known to us the mystery of His will, according to His good pleasure that He planned in Him

10 for the administration of the days of fulfillment—to bring everything together in the Messiah, both things in heaven and things on earth in Him.

18 I pray that the perception of your mind may be enlightened so you may know what is the hope of His calling, what are the glorious riches of His inheritance among the saints,

19 and what is the immeasurable greatness of His power to us who believe, according to the working of His vast strength.

20 He demonstrated this power in the Messiah by raising Him from the dead and seating Him at His right hand in the heavens—

21 far above every ruler and authority, power and dominion, and every title given, not only in this age but also in the one to come.

22 And He put everything under His feet and appointed Him as head over everything for the church,

23 which is His body, the fullness of the One who fills all things in every way.

Mystery (v. 9)—Refers to God's plan for bringing all things and all peoples together through the work of the Messiah, Jesus Christ. This mystery includes the offer of salvation to the Gentiles (see 3:2-13).

Right hand (v. 20)—In the culture of Paul's day, to be seated at the right hand of a king was to be given ultimate authority within the kingdom.

Ephesians 1:7-10

Whenever I pour myself a cup of coffee, I always add cream and mix it together. At that point, a union has occurred. I once had black coffee and white cream, but now I have brown coffee. If I take the coffee with me into my office, the cream comes too. If I take the cream with me into my den, the coffee comes too. Nothing can separate the two once they've been joined.

Likewise, Jesus Christ brings all things together in heaven and on earth. Paul wrote in Colossians, "He is before all things, and by Him all things hold together" (Col. 1:17).

In Jesus, the One who stands exalted like no other, you will discover both the fullness and the summation of everything you'll ever need in heaven and on earth. It's all there—in Him. Everything you need for victorious living is in Jesus.

We so often forfeit Jesus' power and authority simply because we do not remain in Him. Colossians 1:13 tells us God "has rescued us from the domain of darkness and transferred us into the kingdom of the Son He loves." In other words, you used to belong to Satan's kingdom, but now, as a believer, you are part of a new kingdom where Jesus Christ is King. Satan can do nothing to remove you from God's kingdom, but he will do his best to get you to ignore the kingdom rule of Jesus Christ.

Satan is influencing believers' lives because they are yielding the power to him. This is not because of any rightful authority he has, but simply because of a failure to align their thoughts and decisions under the lordship of Jesus Christ. By not exalting Jesus Christ to the proper place in our lives, homes, and churches—the first place He deserves—we miss out on the benefits of His covering.

Do you want the benefits He provides His people? Then remain in Him.

> *What causes us to honor Jesus as Lord in some areas of life but not in others?*

QUESTION **#2**

SHOWING HONOR

Record some of the ways you show honor to the following people. Choose two.

PARENT(S)	SPOUSE	BOSS	GOVERNMENT

What are some ways you can intentionally show honor to Christ?

Ephesians 1:18-21

In a football game, the players tower over the referees. The players are bigger, stronger, and more powerful than the older, smaller, and often out-of-shape referees. In a game, the players can use their power to knock you down—but the referees can use their authority to put you out of the game.

In other words, never confuse power with authority.

Satan may be able to knock you down. He has more power than you. But he has absolutely no authority over you if you're a believer. On the cross, Jesus Christ deactivated, dismantled, and disarmed Satan's rule over sin and death (see Col. 2:13-15). God gave the ultimate authority to His Son. He has placed all things in subjection to Jesus.

Yes, Satan will try long and hard to hinder anyone who has an abiding relationship with Jesus. He wants you to ignore the authority and rule of Christ in your day-to-day activities and decisions. Yet acknowledging and remaining under Christ's lordship and authority will protect you from Satan's onslaught.

Later in Ephesians, Paul wrote that God "made us alive with the Messiah even though we were dead in trespasses. By grace you are saved! He also raised us up with Him and seated us with Him in the heavens, in Christ Jesus" (Eph. 2:5-6).

So, when Christ died, you died with Him. When Christ arose, you arose with Him. When Christ sat down at the right hand of the Father, you sat down with Him. For you to gain access to the authority which comes through the perfect union of Jesus Christ—bringing heaven to bear on earth—you must abide in Him. To abide means to dwell, to align your thoughts, choices, and perspective under God's thoughts, choices, and perspective. It means connecting with Him and honoring Him in everything you do.

> *How do you respond to the truth that Jesus has authority over your everyday life?*
>
> QUESTION **#3**

> *How does acknowledging Jesus' authority over every area of your life benefit you?*
>
> QUESTION **#4**

"Jesus now has many lovers of His heavenly Kingdom, but few bearers of His cross."

—THOMAS À KEMPIS

Ephesians 1:22-23

Because you follow Christ, He now intercedes on your behalf. But the only way to experience His saving power on a daily basis is by aligning yourself under Him. When you do that, you experience the blessings of His care. But know this: experiencing a blessing includes the ability to both enjoy the favor of God in your own life *and* extend His favor to others. We are not "cul-de-sac Christians." We are conduits. God never intended for His blessings to stop at our own lives. He desires for us to be channels through which His blessings will be delivered to others.

Jesus came that we might have life and have it more abundantly (see John 10:10). As we see in Ephesians 1:22-23, He established the church as His own body, of which He is the head. As His body, we are called to serve one another. Love one another. Honor one another. Encourage one another. Forgive one another. Instruct one another. Essentially, we are to reflect and honor Jesus in our words and actions with one another.

Our vertical relationship with God—our intimacy with Him and our access to His authority and blessings—is tied to our horizontal relationship with His body, the church. Because Christ is in us, others should be able to see Jesus in us. He is our head and we as His church, His family of believers, and His body living under His lordship.

We are to function fully under the direction of our head, Jesus Christ. We are to reflect and honor Jesus in all that we do. We are His hands and feet.

What steps can our group take to honor Jesus as head of the church?

QUESTION #5

LIVE IT OUT

How can you honor Jesus with your thoughts, words, and actions? Consider the following suggestions this week:

▶ **Thoughts.** At the end of each day, ask yourself: *Did my thoughts honor the Lord? Or was I preoccupied with myself?*

▶ **Words.** Make it a habit of showing Jesus honor through your words by talking to others with the honor they deserve as people made in His image. Set a goal of avoiding sarcasm and negative speech for a full day.

▶ **Actions.** Keep a journal for one week of how you spend your time. After reviewing your journal, assess if you are honoring Jesus with the first place position in your life.

The life and ministry of Jesus does not end. He is in His rightful and exalted place in heaven—and He is in you. Let His life and ministry flow through the story of your life.

Song: "No Greater Life"

Bible Studies for Life Songs Volume 1 *offers a variety of worship songs based on Bible Studies for Life. As an example, here is the chorus for the song "No Greater Life":*

"Holy God the glorified,
Heaven now in us resides.
Living, breathing, risen Christ;
No greater love, no greater life."

To hear the full song "No Greater Life" from LifeWay Worship, visit *LifeWayWorship.com*.

My group's prayer requests

My thoughts

GENERAL INSTRUCTIONS

In order to make the most of this study and to ensure a richer group experience, it's recommended that all group participants read through the teaching and discussion content in full before each group meeting. As a leader, it is also a good idea for you to be familiar with this content and prepared to summarize it for your group members as you move through the material each week.

Each session of the Bible study is made up of three sections:

1. THE BIBLE MEETS LIFE.

An introduction to the theme of the session and its connection to everyday life, along with a brief overview of the primary Scripture text. This section also includes an icebreaker question or activity.

2. WHAT DOES THE BIBLE SAY?

This comprises the bulk of each session and includes the primary Scripture text along with explanations for key words and ideas within that text. This section also includes most of the content designed to produce and maintain discussion within the group.

3. LIVE IT OUT.

The final section focuses on application, using bulleted summary statements to answer the question, *So what?* As the leader, be prepared to challenge the group to apply what they learned during the discussion by transforming it into action throughout the week.

For group leaders, the *Like No Other* Leader Guide contains several features and tools designed to help you lead participants through the material provided.

QUESTION 1—ICEBREAKER

These opening questions and/or activities are designed to help participants transition into the study and begin engaging the primary themes to be discussed. Be sure everyone has a chance to speak, but maintain a low-pressure environment.

DISCUSSION QUESTIONS

Each "What Does the Bible Say?" section features at least five questions designed to spark discussion and interaction within your group. These questions encourage critical thinking, so be sure to allow a period of silence for participants to process the question and form an answer.

The *Like No Other* Leader Guide also contains follow-up questions and optional activities that may be helpful to your group, if time permits.

DVD CONTENT

Each video features Dr. Tony Evans discussing the primary themes found in the session. We recommend that you show this video in one of three places: (1) At the beginning of group time, (2) After the icebreaker, or (3) After a quick review and/or summary of "What Does the Bible Say?" A video summary is included as well. You may choose to use this summary as background preparation to help you guide the group.

The Leader Guide contains additional questions to help unpack the video and transition into the discussion. For a digital Leader Guide with commentary, see the "Leader Tools" folder on the DVD-ROM in your Leader Kit.

For helps on how to use *Bible Studies for Life*, tips on how to better lead groups, or additional ideas for leading, visit: **www.ministrygrid.com/web/BibleStudiesforLife.**

SESSION 1: PROMISED LIKE NO OTHER

The Point: Jesus is the promised Messiah.

The Passage: Isaiah 53:2-12

The Setting: The prophet Isaiah ministered in the southern kingdom of Judah in the eighth century B.C. during the reigns of kings Uzziah, Jotham, Ahaz, and Hezekiah. Isaiah 53 is the fourth and final of Isaiah's Servant songs or poems about the Suffering Servant, prophecies about the coming Messiah, Jesus. Unlike other messianic prophecies, because these reflect the sufferings of God's Servant, they were not initially understood to be about the Messiah.

QUESTION 1: How do you decide whether someone is believable?

Optional activity: Continue the theme of deception and truthfulness by leading the group in a few rounds of "Two Truths and a Lie." To play, ask for volunteers to offer three statements about themselves—two true and one false. After each volunteer shares his or her statements, encourage group members to guess which is the lie.

Video Summary: In his first video message, Dr. Evans explains a little bit about how the prophecies in the Old Testament predict—years in advance—who Jesus is and what He will do. The book of Isaiah contains prophecies about how God's people will be restored and redeemed and how God will intervene on their behalf. The message can be interpreted as God saying to us, through Isaiah, "I am a God who keeps my promise and here's how I'm going to do it." In Isaiah 53, specifically, we get a picture of the Suffering Servant who came to be the representative of heaven on earth.

WATCH THE DVD SEGMENT FOR SESSION 1, THEN USE THE FOLLOWING QUESTIONS AND DISCUSSION POINTS TO TRANSITION INTO THE STUDY.

- Besides God, in whose promises would you place your trust? Why?
- Has there ever been a time when you regretted believing a promise? Explain.

WHAT DOES THE BIBLE SAY?

ASK FOR A VOLUNTEER TO READ ALOUD ISAIAH 53:2-12.

Response: What's your initial reaction to these verses?

- What do you like about the text?
- What questions do you have about these verses?

TURN THE GROUP'S ATTENTION TO ISAIAH 53:2-3.

QUESTION 2: What surprises you about this description of Christ?

Through answering this question, group members will have an opportunity to examine how their current image of Christ lines up with how this week's Scripture passage describes Him.

Optional follow-up: What words or descriptions in this passage tend to be contrary to our expectations of a great man?

Optional activity: Complete the activity "I Promise!" on page 9. If time permits, encourage volunteers to share the different factors that help them evaluate the promises in God's Word.

MOVE TO ISAIAH 53:4-9.

QUESTION 3: Which prophecies about Jesus in these verses do you find compelling?

This question requires group members to closely examine the biblical text before answering based on how the passage personally impacted them. As time allows, encourage them to explain their responses. Be prepared to offer up a model for the group by answering first.

Optional follow-up: What ideas or images come to mind when you hear the word prophecy?

QUESTION 4: How can you testify to Christ bearing your sickness and carrying your pain?

This question asks group members to recall a personal experience. The objective is for each member to understand, through story, ways in which Christ's sacrifices impact his or her life.

Optional follow-up: In what ways have you been changed because of your encounters with Jesus?

CONTINUE WITH ISAIAH 53:10-12.

QUESTION 5: When have you felt like only Jesus was enough?

This question gives group members another opportunity to share a personal story. The point of this discussion is to help members see that Jesus not only came for us but He has promised to remain with us. To drive home this point you may want to consider spending some time examining Proverbs 18:24 and Psalm 46:1.

Optional follow-up: How can we increase our reliance on Jesus in all situations?

Note: The following question does not appear in the group member book. Use it in your group discussion as time allows.

QUESTION 6: What does this Scripture passage teach us about God's character?

This question is intended to lead group members to identify what they can know about who God is based on the words of this text.

LIVE IT OUT

Encourage group members to consider taking the following steps to strengthen their faith:

- **Discover God's promises.** As you read the Bible, highlight any verses that contain a promise from God.
- **Trust His plan.** Make it a point to actively proclaim your trust in God each day. When you pray, acknowledge His plan for your life and declare your intention to trust Him.
- **Search His prophecies.** Use a Bible dictionary or concordance to look up Old Testament prophecies about Jesus. Consider how each prophecy underscores the truth of who Jesus is.

Challenge: Don't allow yourself to simply notice the promises contained in God's Word. Rather, when you come across God's promises this week, commit to believing them as truth. Consider writing them down as you encounter them and putting them in a place where you will see them and be reminded often.

Pray: Ask for prayer requests and ask group members to pray for the different requests as intercessors. As the leader, close this time by asking the Lord to help each of you remember that He not only came for us but also remains with us as our lifeline and assurance. Thank Him for keeping His promises.

SESSION 2: A BIRTH LIKE NO OTHER

The Point: Jesus is fully human and fully God.

The Passage: Luke 1:26-35

The Setting: Luke wrote his two-volume work (Luke and Acts) for the purpose of demonstrating the spread of the gospel beyond the Jewish world and to the world as a whole. But before he could focus on the spread of the gospel (Acts), he had to demonstrate the reality of the good news of the gospel (Luke). He began that endeavor by addressing the birth of John the Baptist, who first spread the word about Jesus, and the birth of Jesus Himself.

QUESTION 1: How do you typically introduce yourself to someone new?

The goal of this question is for group members to share what types of information they reveal about themselves when they first meet someone new— to identify what information they view as most important when expressing who they are.

Optional activity: Enhance your group members' engagement with "The Bible Meets Life" by passing around several pictures of newborn babies. You can find such pictures in your own family archives or by searching through magazines and other forms of media. Remember that images are a great way to help visual learners become more invested in a discussion experience.

Video Summary: In this video session, Dr. Evans walks us through what it means that our Savior is 100 percent God and 100 percent man. As God He can address anything. As man He can identify with anything that needs to be addressed. As man He can feel our pain. As God He can soothe our pain. As man He can cry. As God He can wipe tears. God and man are brought together by the unique birth of the Perfect Man. The Man who can redeem mankind. The God-Man.

WATCH THE DVD SEGMENT FOR SESSION 2, THEN USE THE FOLLOWING QUESTIONS AND DISCUSSION POINTS TO TRANSITION INTO THE STUDY.

- In what ways do you think Jesus being fully human helps Him meet your needs?
- How does the fact that Jesus was both fully God and fully human impact your faith?

WHAT DOES THE BIBLE SAY?

ASK FOR A VOLUNTEER TO READ ALOUD LUKE 1:26-35.

Response: What's your initial reaction to these verses?

- What questions do you have about these verses?
- What do you hope to gain from studying about what it means the Jesus was both fully God and fully human?

TURN THE GROUP'S ATTENTION TO LUKE 1:26-31.

QUESTION 2: Since Jesus existed before time, why is it significant that He came as a baby?

This question requires group members to go a step beyond interpreting the biblical text and to understanding the significance of the One who, even from the time and method of conception, was already both fully human and fully divine.

Optional follow-up: How would you explain in your own words why Jesus was born of a virgin?

MOVE TO LUKE 1:32-33.

QUESTION 3: What are the differences between living in a democracy and living under Jesus as the Sovereign Ruler?

This question provides an opportunity for group members to define for themselves what it means to do life in our culture while operating from a place of submission to a Sovereign Ruler who reigns now and for all eternity in the lives of those who follow Him. You may also want to look as a group at Galatians 3:28.

CONTINUE WITH LUKE 1:34-35.

QUESTION 4: Since Jesus lived as a man, why is it important to understand He is God?

As you discuss this question, consider drawing the group's attention back to The Point for this session. Guide group members to consider first why it is significant that Jesus lived for a time as a man. Then help them transition to the importance of understanding that He was and is also fully God and what that means in our lives today and for eternity.

Optional follow-up: What does our culture teach about Jesus' nature and identity?

Optional activity: Encourage group members to complete the activity "Double Encouragement" on page 21. As time allows, invite volunteers to share their responses to what they find encouraging about Jesus' human nature and His divine nature.

QUESTION 5: Jesus is fully God and fully man. How does that truth influence your choices this week?

This question is designed to help group members work through what it looks like practically to live out the significance of Jesus being fully God and fully man in their day-to-day lives. Encourage them to listen closely as others share. They can learn much from the responses of other members of the group.

Optional follow-up: What responsibilities do you carry based on your knowledge of Jesus?

Note: The following question does not appear in the group member book. Use it in your group discussion as time allows.

QUESTION 6: How have you personally come to an understanding of who Jesus is?

The question gives members an opportunity to share with the group what they believe about who God is through their own personal experiences.

Optional follow-up: How can you take your personal experience and help someone else understand who Jesus is? Be specific.

LIVE IT OUT

Invite group members to take one of the following steps in response to the truth that Jesus is fully human and fully God:

- **Dig deeper.** Ask your pastor to recommend a book, article, or podcast that can help you better understand Jesus' nature.
- **Get to know God's Word.** Meditate on Jesus' divinity and humanity by memorizing Hebrews 4:15-16 over the next few days. Concentrate on the truths those verses express.
- **Invite someone to know Jesus.** Pray for an opportunity to talk with someone who may not realize Jesus is both fully human and fully God. Be honest and encouraging as you share the truth of God's Word.

Challenge: Don't be afraid to stand for the truth of Jesus' identity and character. Look for opportunities this week to share examples from your own personal journey that illustrate Jesus as fully God and fully human. And when those opportunities present themselves, be ready and willing to do so.

Pray: Ask for prayer requests and ask group members to pray for the different requests as intercessors. As the leader, close this time by committing the members of your group to the Lord and asking Him to help each of you live fully out of the knowledge that He came to earth as the Son of God so that we could know God and experience Him more fully.

SESSION 3: POWER LIKE NO OTHER

The Point: Jesus has power over all my fears.

The Passage: Mark 4:35-41

The Setting: This passage in Mark's Gospel is the first of a collection of four miracle accounts (4:35–5:43) that immediately follow a separate collection of parables (4:1-34). It is as if the Gospel is validating the teachings of Jesus in those parables by following them up with demonstrations of His authority over nature, demons, death, and disease. With such comprehensive authority, why should my fears prove any challenge to Him?

QUESTION 1: What forms of power really get your attention?

Optional activity: Bring a whiteboard or a large sheet of paper to the group meeting. As a lead-in to Question 1, ask group members to think of every possible definition or expression of the word power. Ask a volunteer to record each answer and group them according to categories, if possible. When finished, offer the final list as a springboard for possible answers to Question 1.

Video Summary: In this video session, Dr. Evans talks about the power available to us when we are connected to Jesus Christ. We can call forth His power and rest in it. He has overcome the world, and because of His power in us, we can overcome as well. Satan tries to use situations to drive us from the Lord. The Lord wants to use situations to drive us to Him. His power can override whatever this world lays at our feet.

WATCH THE DVD SEGMENT FOR SESSION 3, THEN USE THE FOLLOWING QUESTIONS AND DISCUSSION POINTS TO TRANSITION INTO THE STUDY.

- What is required to weather a storm well?
- Share with the group a specific time when His power changed you in the midst of a difficulty.

WHAT DOES THE BIBLE SAY?
ASK FOR A VOLUNTEER TO READ ALOUD MARK 4:35-41.

Response: What's your initial reaction to these verses?
- What questions do you have about these verses?
- What new application do you hope to get from this passage?

TURN THE GROUP'S ATTENTION TO MARK 4:35-38a.

QUESTION 2: In what ways do we typically respond to frightening situations?

This question is designed to help group members consider how people (themselves as well as others) tend to react to their fear. Answers will vary based on individual experiences.

Optional follow-up: When have you felt like God was unconcerned with your problems?

MOVE TO MARK 4:38b-39.

QUESTION 3: How have you learned that God really does care about His people?

This question will allow group members an opportunity to share personal stories as well as acknowledge and reflect on how their lives have been affected by God's care for them.

Optional follow-up: In what ways can you use what you have learned to help someone who doubts that God really cares?

QUESTION 4: How can we reconcile the truth of Jesus' power with the fact that He doesn't always calm the storm?

This question is designed to give group members permission to struggle with the tension that results from knowing that Jesus has the power to calm the storm but doesn't always choose to do so. Encourage them to be honest with their questions and answers, but make sure you draw the discussion back to the truth of who Jesus is and what He promises His followers.

Optional activity: Direct group members to complete the activity "All My Fears" on page 31. If time permits, ask for volunteers to share which image they chose.

CONTINUE WITH MARK 4:40-41.

QUESTION 5: In your everyday life, what does it mean to respond to Jesus' power?

This question differs from a broad perspective on what Jesus' power means for our lives and encourages group members to consider what His power looks like for them in the day-to-day. Encourage specific and practical responses.

Optional follow-up: What obstacles prevent us from responding to His power?

Note: The following question does not appear in the group member book. Use it in your group discussion as time allows.

QUESTION 6: How do we bridge the gap between knowing about faith and demonstrating faith?

Encourage group members to do some self-examination before they respond. As time allows, also invite them to share actions steps for moving forward in demonstrating faith.

LIVE IT OUT

Encourage group members to consider the following ways they can let go of fear and trust in Jesus' power:

- **Write it down.** Make a list of the most pressing external problems that give rise to your internal fears. Pray over this list in connection with the trust found in John 16:33.
- **Watch your words.** Each day, assess whether your speech is more focused on your problems or on Jesus, who is the solution. Seek to speak more openly about Jesus.
- **Pray together.** Consider ways you can encourage others to trust Christ. Look for evidence of people struggling with turmoil and invite them to pray with you for peace.

Challenge: Many times we don't know how much faith we have until our faith gets tested. Be on alert this week for times when your faith is tested and take notice of how you react. Ask the Lord to make you aware of those times and what you need to learn through them.

Pray: Ask for prayer requests and ask group members to pray for the different requests as intercessors. As the leader, close this time by acknowledging that when we face uneasy times, we don't have to feel powerless or overwhelmed because we know the One who has what we need. Thank Him for His power and His willingness to use that power on our behalf.

SESSION 4: TEACHINGS LIKE NO OTHER

The Point: Jesus teaches us how to live and calls us to follow Him.

The Passage: Mark 1:21-22; 10:17-22

The Setting: Mark 1:21-22 occurs early in Jesus' ministry. He had completed 40 days in the wilderness, John the Baptist had been arrested, and Jesus had called Peter, Andrew, and John to follow Him when they entered a synagogue in Capernaum and Jesus began to teach. Mark again records Jesus teaching in the latter part of Mark 9 (in Capernaum) and the early part of Mark 10 (in Judea). Against the backdrop of Jesus' teaching, a man approached the Teacher to ask a question.

QUESTION 1: What makes your favorite teacher your favorite teacher?

Optional activity: To continue the theme of teaching, ask for volunteers to teach the group something interesting. Request that volunteers be brief, using no more than two minutes each if possible. Ideas for teaching could include offering tips for a smartphone, explaining how something works, recounting a piece of trivia they recently learned, sharing their professional expertise, and so on.

Note: You will likely have time for two or three volunteers, depending on how long each person takes to teach. Also, it would be best to communicate this opportunity to group members prior to the gathering so they can prepare.

Video Summary: This week Dr. Evans talks about the greatest teacher of all time—Jesus Christ. This great Teacher always taught absolute truth. He taught where the people were, but He never compromised truth. His message came out of a heart of love and a desire to help. He is the final word and authority in the life of every believer. And He provided a way for us to experience His teaching today through the Bible— the voice of Jesus in print. We have full access to His truth, and what we choose to do with that truth will determine what our tomorrow looks like.

WATCH THE DVD SEGMENT FOR SESSION 4, THEN USE THE FOLLOWING QUESTIONS AND DISCUSSION POINTS TO TRANSITION INTO THE STUDY.
- Who has been most influential in teaching you the truth of Scripture? Explain.
- In what ways have you invested in others to share that same truth with them?

WHAT DOES THE BIBLE SAY?
ASK FOR A VOLUNTEER TO READ ALOUD
MARK 1:21-22; 10:17-22.
Response: What's your initial reaction to these verses?
- What do you like about the text?
- What new application do you hope to receive about what it truly means to live life to the fullest?

TURN THE GROUP'S ATTENTION TO
MARK 1:21-22.
QUESTION 2: What's the difference between knowledge and authority?
This question is designed to give group members an opportunity to define for themselves two terms that will influence their understanding of this week's biblical text.
Optional follow-up: How do we express and encounter authority in today's culture?

Optional activity: Direct group members to complete the activity "Assessment: Jesus' Teaching" on page 39. Encourage volunteers to share their reactions to the assessment.

MOVE TO MARK 10:17-21a.
QUESTION 3: How does Jesus' approach help us love those we disagree with?
The question requires that group members interpret this Scripture passage for themselves as a way to move them toward life application.
Optional follow-up: Share one situation in which you can put this teaching into practice this week.

CONTINUE WITH MARK 10:21b-22.
QUESTION 4: Why is it loving for Jesus to call us to do something difficult or even painful?
This question is designed to help group members recognize that Jesus' teaching calls for a response. When a situation requires us to make a choice about our obedience, our decision demonstrates to ourselves and to Him what it is we truly believe.
Optional follow-up: What obstacles are hindering you from more fully obeying Christ?

QUESTION 5: How have Jesus' teachings changed the way you live?

This question provides group members an opportunity to share specific instances of positive change in their lives. As they share their responses, encourage members to also share examples of how they lived before His truth changed things.

Optional follow-up: Which of Jesus' teachings would you like to focus on as you continue to grow spiritually?

Note: The following question does not appear in the group member book. Use it in your group discussion as time allows.

QUESTION 6: When have you been surprised by God's answer to your question?

This question invites member of the group to share their personal testimonies of how they have experienced God in their lives in unexpected ways.

LIVE IT OUT

Invite group members to consider the following ways they can apply Jesus' teaching to their daily lives:

- **Read.** Read through one of the Gospels this week. As you come across Jesus' different teachings, reflect on how living by that teaching would benefit your life.
- **Commit.** As you read God's Word, make a conscious, deliberate decision to obey what it teaches. Pray through that commitment for the rest of the day.
- **Teach.** Consider leading a Bible study or teaching a class for kids, students, or adults. Let God use you to communicate the teachings of Jesus to others.

Challenge: Remember that it's never enough to read, understand, and believe Jesus' teachings. Obedience is a necessary requirement. Therefore, intentionally identify one of Jesus' teachings that you will put in practice each day this week.

Pray: Ask for prayer requests and ask group members to pray for the different requests as intercessors. As the leader, close this time by asking the Lord to help each of you look to Him to learn how to live well—to learn what it means to live life to the fullest. Thank Him for the opportunity we have to sit as His feet and learn everyday.

SESSION 5: A DEATH LIKE NO OTHER

The Point: Jesus' death is the heart of the gospel.

The Passage: Matthew 27:28-31,45-50,54

The Setting: Jesus had completed His earthly ministry save His justifying death and victorious resurrection. He had been arrested in Gethsemane, railroaded through a sham trial of the Sanhedrin, falsely accused before Pilate, and rejected by the crowd in favor of the notorious prisoner Barabbas. At that point, Pilate released Barabbas, had Jesus flogged, and turned Him over to the soldiers to be crucified.

QUESTION 1: Why do we care when famous people pass away?

Optional activity: Use an object lesson to emphasize the reality of Jesus' physical death throughout your discussion. Bring a dead or dying plant to the gathering and display it in a place everyone can see. As you read the record of Jesus' death, use the plant as a way to reinforce the fact that His physical body perished. He literally died for us.

Note: If you don't have any houseplants that are dead or dying, consider looking through the sale racks at your local garden shop or home-improvement store.

Video Summary: In this session, Dr. Evans spends time walking through some weighty theological terms—sin, grace, justification, redemption, propitiation, reconciliation—in explaining how God sent Jesus as our eternal substitute to pay the penalty for the sins of the whole world. "He made the One who did not know sin to be sin for us, so that we might become the righteousness of God in Him" (2 Cor. 5:21). The Son of God paid the price to secure our eternal destiny. He took on hell for us on the cross—truly a death like no other.

WATCH THE DVD SEGMENT FOR SESSION 5, THEN USE THE FOLLOWING QUESTIONS AND DISCUSSION POINTS TO TRANSITION INTO THE STUDY.

- When has someone sacrificed for you? What impact has their sacrifice had on you?
- When have you sacrificed for another? What impact has your sacrifice had on you?

WHAT DOES THE BIBLE SAY?

ASK FOR A VOLUNTEER TO READ ALOUD MATTHEW 27:28-31,45-50,54.

Response: What's your initial reaction to these verses?
- What questions do you have about these verses?
- What new application do you hope to get from this passage?

TURN THE GROUP'S ATTENTION TO MATTHEW 27:28-31.

QUESTION 2: What do these verses teach us about Jesus?

This question asks member to look beyond the words of this passage to discover what can be learned about Jesus.

Optional follow-up: What are some ways we mistreat Jesus today?

MOVE TO MATTHEW 27:45-50.

QUESTION 3: How do we explore the tension between the truth of God's love and the events in these verses?

This question is meant to first acknowledge that there is a tension present between what we know about God's love and what is happening to Jesus in these verses. Be willing to manage this tension while you discuss how it can be navigated.

Optional follow-up: Why is it important to understand that Jesus actually died?

QUESTION 4: What emotions have you experienced while discussing Jesus' death?

Remind group members that there is no "correct" answer to this question. You're asking them to be open and honest about the feelings they have experienced as they have come face to face with the realization of the ultimate sacrifice Jesus made for us.

Optional follow-up: What are some ways you'd like to respond after this reminder of Jesus' death on your behalf?

CONTINUE WITH MATTHEW 27:54.

QUESTION 5: When in your own life did you encounter the truth that Jesus is God's Son?

This question calls for a personal story, but some members in the room could be encountering this truth for the very first time. Hopefully they will consider your group a safe place to ask questions they may have been reluctant to ask in the past. Be prepared to start this discussion yourself if group members seem hesitant.

Optional follow-up: The centurion concluded that Jesus is the Son of God. What other conclusions do people make?

Note: The following question does not appear in the group member book. Use it in your group discussion as time allows.

QUESTION 6: Why is Jesus' death the heart of the gospel?

This question calls for application based on the biblical text and is designed to make sure group members conclude this session with an understanding of the true importance of Jesus' death and the implication His sacrifice has for the lives of all believers.

LIVE IT OUT

Encourage group members to consider the following options for responding to what Jesus' death means in their lives:

- **Confess.** Ask God to forgive you of your sins in light of Jesus' death on the cross.
- **Show gratitude.** Set aside time each day to intentionally express gratitude to Jesus for the sacrifice He made on your behalf. Let that gratitude influence your words and actions.
- **Invite others.** Invite someone to join you next week as your group discusses what happened after Jesus died on the cross. The focus on Christ's resurrection is a great time to introduce someone to the gospel.

Challenge: Christians can be passive when it comes to sharing the good news of the gospel. Choose to be proactive this week by initiating a spiritual conversation and proclaiming the message of salvation to someone who needs to hear it.

Pray: Ask for prayer requests and ask group members to pray for the different requests as intercessors. As the leader, close by asking the Lord to help each of you ground your lives in what it means that Jesus died on the cross for us. Thank Him for the sacrifice He made.

SESSION 6: RESURRECTED LIKE NO OTHER

The Point: Jesus is alive—and we can live forever.

The Passage: Matthew 28:1-10

The Setting: Jesus' torturous death on the cross had ended His physical suffering, but His followers' emotional suffering had only begun. For three terrifying, dreadful days, those followers grappled unsuccessfully trying to make sense out of His brutal death, seeking any insight to reconcile their expectations for Jesus to the new reality without Him. Then Mary Magdalene and Mary went to the tomb to anoint His body.

QUESTION 1: When were you excited to experience something firsthand?

Optional activity: Bring several small rocks or pebbles to the group gathering. Distribute a rock to each group member and explain that the rocks represent the stone the angel rolled away from Jesus' tomb. Encourage members to carry the stones in their pockets or purses as a reminder that Jesus was physically resurrected from the dead—and that the evidence of His resurrection was seen by many witnesses.

Video Summary: In this session, Dr. Evans talks about the good news of the resurrection and its importance for believers. The resurrection means that the price for our sins was paid, received, and accepted. This is the security and assurance for our eternal destiny. His resurrection affirms that death no longer has the last say for all who have placed faith in Him. His resurrection has eternal significance but we don't have to wait until heaven to reap the benefits—Jesus

Christ rose from the dead and has been transforming lives ever since. He forgives, changes weaknesses to strengths, reverses the course of lives, guides decision-making. He is what we need when we need it.

WATCH THE DVD SEGMENT FOR SESSION 6, THEN USE THE FOLLOWING QUESTIONS AND DISCUSSION POINTS TO TRANSITION INTO THE STUDY.

- What do you think it is about anticipating death that makes us fearful?
- How might a Christian's life reflect what he or she believes about Jesus' resurrection?

WHAT DOES THE BIBLE SAY?

ASK FOR A VOLUNTEER TO READ ALOUD MATTHEW 28:1-10.

Response: What's your initial reaction to these verses?

- What questions do you have about the meaning of the resurrection?
- What new application do you hope to get from this passage?

TURN THE GROUP'S ATTENTION TO MATTHEW 28:1-7.

QUESTION 2: Why does it matter that Jesus physically rose from the dead?

We often settle for the "what" without drilling down to understand the "why." This question will provide that opportunity. Guide the discussion to help group members understand the significance of needing a risen Savior in whom to place our living faith.

Optional follow-up: What evidence of Jesus' resurrection do you find most convincing? Why?

QUESTION 3: In what ways has Jesus' resurrection impacted history?

This question gives group members an opportunity to look beyond how Jesus' resurrection has impacted their lives personally and consider the broader impact on history. Guide them to consider how the influence of His sacrifice on individual lives has impacted history through the church, society, etc.

Optional follow-up: In what ways have you witnessed the power of Christ?

CONTINUE WITH MATTHEW 28:8-10.

QUESTION 4: Why is worship still the appropriate response to the resurrection?

Answering this question will require group members to define for themselves what worship means and why they see it as important. Consider closing this discussion by reading together Psalm 95:1-6.

Optional activity: Direct group members to complete the activity "Worship Him" on page 57.

QUESTION 5: How will Jesus' resurrection impact your life in the days to come?

This question requires group members to develop an intentional action plan for their lives based on the meaning of the resurrection. It promotes accountability and the need to act on biblical truth.

Note: The following question does not appear in the group member book. Use it in your group discussion as time allows.

QUESTION 6: What can we learn from the repeated presence of fear in these verses?

This question asks group members to interpret the biblical text for their own lives. Encourage them to look beyond the words for godly principles.

Optional follow-up: In what ways can you put those lessons to work in facing your own fears this week?

LIVE IT OUT

Encourage group members to consider the following suggestions of ways to respond to the hope of Jesus' resurrection:

- **Seek peace.** Too many people allow the fear of the future to hold them back. Ask the Holy Spirit to help you embrace the peace that comes with eternal life through Christ.
- **Celebrate!** Jesus' resurrection remains the best news anyone can hear. Therefore, make a concerted effort to celebrate that miracle this week. Give yourself permission to feel joy.
- **Pay it forward.** Someone told you about the gift of eternal life available in Christ. Do the same for someone else by explaining how they can have future hope in Christ.

Challenge: The message of the resurrection is that you and I can have the promise of eternal life. We can live forever and love forever. Such good news should affect what we do each day. Being mindful of this truth, make plans to take one action each day this week to live out the hope you have because of the resurrection.

Pray: Ask for prayer requests and ask group members to pray for the different requests as intercessors. As the leader, close this time by thanking the Lord for the miracle of love that was illustrated in the resurrection. Close your time by worshipping Him through the words of the psalmist in Psalm 95:1-6.

SESSION 7: ASCENDED LIKE NO OTHER

The Point: Jesus ascended to heaven but did not leave us alone.

The Passage: Acts 1:3-11

The Setting: Jewish officials did their best spin doctoring in their effort to control and shape the message about the empty tomb. But, they had no control over the resurrected Jesus. Over a 40-day period, Jesus appeared numerous times to various individuals and groups, presumably to encourage them and to teach them those things they had not been ready to learn before the crucifixion. At the end of 40 days, Jesus had one final appearance and word of instruction before returning to the Father in heaven.

QUESTION 1: Whose words always catch your attention?

Optional activity: We can say that Jesus "did not leave us alone" because of the Holy Spirit's presence in our lives. However, we aren't always aware of the Spirit's work and influence. As a way of illustrating the Spirit's presence, bring a portable fan to the group meeting. Before moving into the main portion of this session, turn the fan to a low setting and position it so that group members experience a light breeze. Explain that the breeze should serve as a reminder of the Holy Spirit's presence as you continue studying the life of Jesus.

Video Summary: In this video message, Dr. Evans explains why Jesus ascended. Before He left, Jesus gathered His disciples to explain to them that in His absence He would be leaving someone to act in His place. While Jesus was on earth, He functioned where He was geographically. When He ascended, He sent His Holy Spirit to indwell and empower His followers who would then infiltrate the world with the good news of the gospel. Through the ascension of Jesus Christ, we are able to experience His unique spiritual presence and power.

WATCH THE DVD SEGMENT FOR SESSION 7, THEN USE THE FOLLOWING QUESTIONS AND DISCUSSION POINTS TO TRANSITION INTO THE STUDY.

- After watching the video message, in what way do you have a better understanding of Jesus' ascension?
- Which word do you think best describes Jesus' ascension—sad, hopeful, confusing, or amazing? Explain your answer.

WHAT DOES THE BIBLE SAY?

ASK FOR A VOLUNTEER TO READ ALOUD ACTS 1:3-11.

Response: What's your initial reaction to these verses?
- What do you like about the text?
- What questions do you have about these verses?

TURN THE GROUP'S ATTENTION TO ACTS 1:3.

QUESTION 2: If you had a limited time with Jesus, what would you most want to learn?

Another way to phrase this question would be: "If you could have Jesus teach you one thing, what would it be?" As time allows, encourage group members to explain their answers.

Optional follow-up: What have you learned or heard about the kingdom of God?

MOVE TO ACTS 1:4-8.

QUESTION 3: In your own words, how would you describe the presence and work of the Holy Spirit?

This question provides group members with an opportunity to articulate the meaning of the presence and work of the Holy Spirit. This activity will help them better define the concept for themselves as well as prepare them to share it with others.

Optional activity: Direct group members to complete the activity "Plugged In?" on page 67. If time permits, ask volunteers to share what helps them connect with the Spirit's power each day.

CONTINUE WITH ACTS 1:9-11.

QUESTION 4: Why is it important that Jesus' disciples witnessed His ascension?

This question allows group members an opportunity to process, through the filter of the biblical text, why Jesus felt it was important for His disciples to experience His ascension firsthand. Guide group members to consider the importance seeing the ascension played in the disciple's understanding of Jesus' heavenly position.

QUESTION 5: How does the promise of Jesus' return influence your daily decisions?

This question is designed to help group members apply the truth of the biblical text to their everyday lives and to make adjustments or put into place a more intentional plan if necessary.

Optional follow-up: What emotions do you experience when you think about Jesus' return?

Note: The following question does not appear in the group member book. Use it in your group discussion as time allows.

QUESTION 6: What questions would you like to ask or discuss about the role of the Holy Spirit in our world?

Hopefully group members will feel comfortable enough in your group to ask questions they may have. Be willing to start this discussion yourself to help others feel more comfortable. It's likely both believers and non-believers have or have had questions regarding the role of the Holy Spirit, but be sensitive to non-Christians who may be in the group.

Optional follow-up: In what ways do you now feel better equipped to call on the power of the Holy Spirit in your life?

LIVE IT OUT

Invite members to consider the following options for responding to Jesus' ascension and eventual return:

- **Plug in.** Begin each day by asking the Holy Spirit to make Himself known in your life. Pray that He will offer clear directions as you weigh options and make decisions.
- **Research.** Look through articles, sermons, podcasts, or books in order to broaden your understanding of the Holy Spirit and His role in your life.
- **Let go.** Our future is in heaven with Jesus. Therefore, choose to let go of something—a possession, a grudge, a way of life—that keeps you tethered to this world.

Challenge: Consider using a physical object to remind yourself about the Holy Spirit's presence in your life this week. Wear a wristband, for example, or carry something in your pocket that symbolizes the Spirit's presence.

Pray: Ask for prayer requests and ask group members to pray for the different requests. As the leader, close by asking the Lord to help each of you remember that even though Jesus ascended to heaven, He did not leave us alone. Thank Him for the gift of the Holy Spirit.

SESSION 8: EXALTED LIKE NO OTHER

The Point: Honor Jesus as Lord.

The Passage: Ephesians 1:7-10,18-23

The Setting: As Paul wrote to the Ephesian believers, he doesn't seem to have been addressing any particular local theological or moral problems. He had already spent three years in the city on his third missionary journey, and the church there had already benefited from the ministries of Aquila and Priscilla as well as Apollos. Rather than intervening in problem areas, Paul wrote to emphasize the significance of the believers as the body of Christ, and began by stressing the blessings believers have in Christ.

QUESTION 1: What's your favorite way to honor others?
Optional activity: Emphasize the theme of honoring others by using your group meeting as

a venue to honor someone known by most group members. For example, you could honor your pastor or another member of your church staff. Or you could honor a group member who has a birthday coming up, just got a promotion, has been in the group longest, and so on. Bring food, say something kind, and help group members get a taste of what it means to show honor to someone else—all as a way to help them think through what it means to honor Jesus as Lord.

Note: Be sure to plan ahead for this celebration. Attempting something spontaneous could backfire in several ways.

Video Summary: In this closing session, Dr. Evans explains God's intention that all of life and history revolve around His Son, Jesus Christ. And, in turn, our lives are to revolve around Him as well. When God's philosophy about Jesus becomes our philosophy about Jesus, we will experience more of Him because we are being ruled by Him. When we exalt the Son of God by making Him Lord in our lives, we have access to the riches of the Father.

WATCH THE DVD SEGMENT FOR SESSION 8, THEN USE THE FOLLOWING QUESTIONS AND DISCUSSION POINTS TO TRANSITION INTO THE STUDY.

- In your opinion, what does the life of someone who exalts the Lord look like? Be specific.
- What is it about your life that makes others want to know Jesus?

WHAT DOES THE BIBLE SAY?
ASK FOR A VOLUNTEER TO READ ALOUD
EPHESIANS 1:7-10,18-23.
Response: What's your initial reaction to these verses?
- What questions do you have about these verses?
- What do you hope to gain from learning what it means to honor the Lord?

TURN THE GROUP'S ATTENTION TO EPHESIANS 1:7-10.
QUESTION 2: What causes us to honor Jesus as Lord in some areas of life but not in others?

Identifying difficulties and barriers associated with honoring Jesus as Lord should move members along a continuum that culminates with discovering how they can better live lives that honor Him in everything.

Optional follow-up: How have you experienced the blessings described in this passage?

Optional activity: Direct group members to complete the activity "Showing Honor" on page 77. If time permits, encourage volunteers to share how they honor people in different roles.

MOVE TO EPHESIANS 1:18-21.

QUESTION 3: How do you respond to the truth that Jesus has authority over your everyday life?

The intent of this question is to prompt interaction with the biblical text and reveal attitudes and conclusions that may have prevented members from considering how Jesus' authority impacts their lives in the day-to-day.

Optional follow-up: How is the lordship of Jesus different from the role of a boss or a CEO?

QUESTION 4: How does acknowledging Jesus' authority over every area of your life benefit you?

This question is intended to help group members make the connection between doing what is asked of us as believers—to honor Jesus as Lord— and the benefits we receive from doing so. You may want to spend some time talking about such benefits as "the glorious riches of His inheritance" (v. 18) and "the immeasurable greatness of His power" (v. 19).

CONTINUE WITH EPHESIANS 1:22-23.

QUESTION 5: What steps can our group take to honor Jesus as head of the church?

Encourage group members to be specific in working together to answer this question. What *practical* steps can your group take to honor Jesus as head of the church?

Optional follow-up: What steps can we take as individuals?

Note: The following question does not appear in the group member book. Use it in your group discussion as time allows.

QUESTION 6: When are we often tempted to honor something or someone other than Jesus as Lord of our lives?

What we say we believe isn't always the truest indicator of what we really believe. The truest indicator of what we believe is behavior. This question asks the group to consider instances when their behavior may reveal something other than what they think they believe about God. The follow-up question will help them develop a plan for change if necessary.

Optional follow-up: What intentional actions can you take moving forward to make sure you aren't tempted to misplace your honor?

LIVE IT OUT

Invite group members to consider the following ways they can honor Jesus with their thoughts, words, and actions:

- **Thoughts.** At the end of each day, ask yourself: *Did my thoughts honor the Lord? Or was I preoccupied with myself?*
- **Words.** Make it a habit of showing Jesus honor through your words by talking to others with the honor they deserve as people made in His image. Set a goal of avoiding sarcasm and negative speech for a full day.
- **Actions.** Keep a journal for one week of how you spend your time. After reviewing your journal, assess if you are honoring Jesus with the first place position in your life.

Challenge: The life and ministry of Jesus does not end. He is in His rightful and exalted place in heaven—and He is in you. Take some time this week to read and meditate on Ephesians 2:5-6 and allow His story to flow through the story of your life.

Pray: As the leader, close this final session of *Like No Other* in prayer. Ask the Lord to help each of you continue to live out the reality of who He is and the truths learned in this study. Conclude by committing to let His life and ministry flow through the story of your life.

WHERE THE BIBLE MEETS LIFE

Bible Studies for Life™ will help you know Christ, live in community, and impact the world around you. If you enjoyed this study, be sure and check out these other available titles.* Six sessions each.

Pressure Points *by Chip Henderson*

When Relationships Collide *by Ron Edmondson*

Do Over: Experience New Life in Christ *by Ben Mandrell*

Honest to God: Real Questions People Ask *by Robert Jeffress*

Let Hope In *by Pete Wilson*

Productive: Finding Joy in What We Do *by Ronnie and Nick Floyd*

Connected: My Life in the Church *by Thom S. Rainer*

Resilient Faith: Standing Strong in the Midst of Suffering *by Mary Jo Sharp*

Beyond Belief: Exploring the Character of God *by Freddy Cardoza*

Overcome: Living Beyond Your Circumstances *by Alex Himaya*

Storm Shelter: God's Embrace in the Psalms *by Philip Nation*

Ready: Ministering to Those in Crisis *by Chip Ingram*

If your group meets regularly, you might consider Bible Studies for Life as an ongoing series. Available for your entire church—kids, students, and adults—it's a format that will be a more affordable option over time. And you can jump in anytime. For more information, visit **biblestudiesforlife.com**.

biblestudiesforlife.com/smallgroups
800.458.2772 | LifeWay Christian Stores

Additional titles will continue to be released every three months.
Visit website for more information.

LifeWay
Biblical Solutions for Life

Learning about Circles

This is a **circle**.

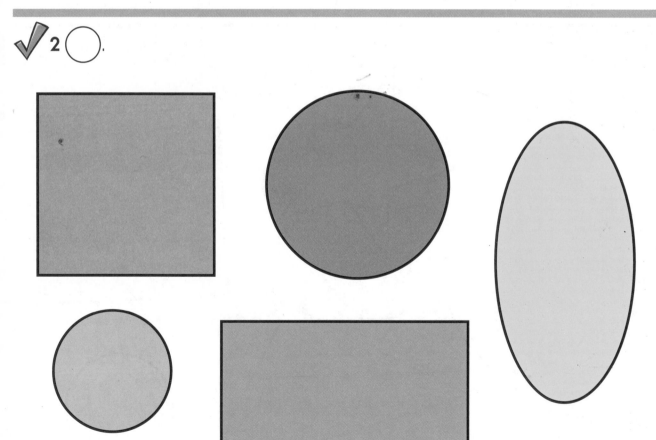

✓ 2 ◯.

Color the ◯.

Color **2** ◯.

Finding & Coloring a Circle

Color the ◯ orange.

✏️ Trace all the ◯.

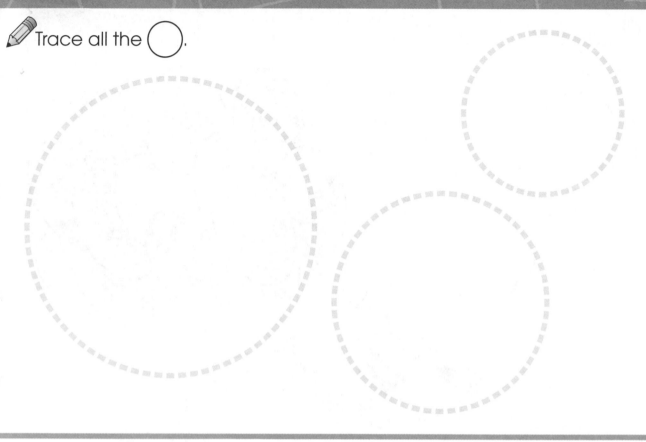

✏️ Finish the ◯. Then draw a ◯.

 all the ◯ in the picture.

How many ◯ did you find? **5 6 7**

This is a **square**.

✓ 2 ☐.

Coloring Squares

Color the ☐.

Color 2 ☐.

Finding & Coloring a Square

Color the ☐ red.

Tracing & Drawing Squares

Trace all the ☐.

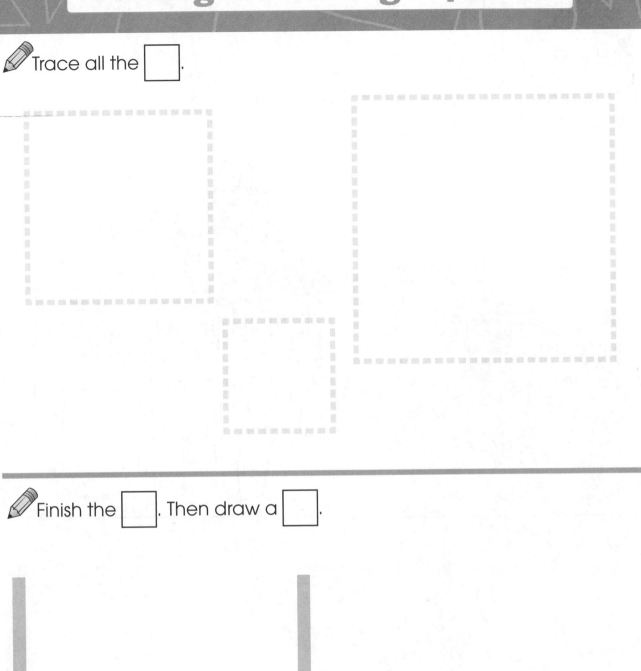

Finish the ☐. Then draw a ☐.

Square Search

✓ all the ☐ in the picture.

✏ How many ☐ did you find? **5 6 7**

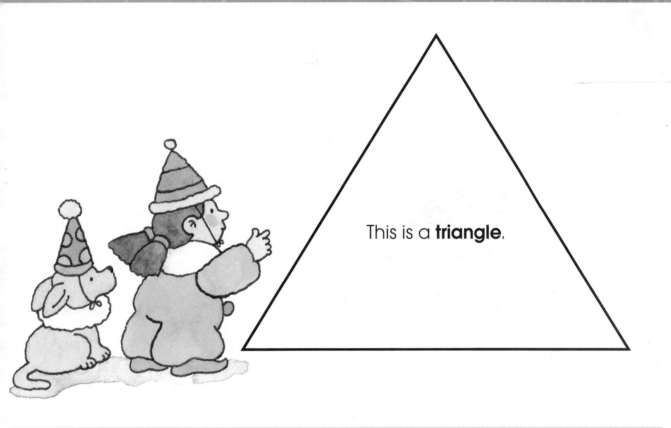

This is a **triangle**.

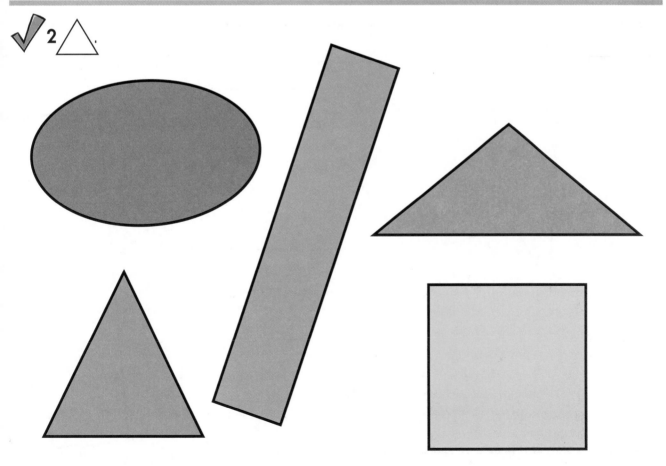

Coloring Triangles

Color the △.

Color **2** △.

Finding & Coloring a Triangle

Color the △ yellow.

Tracing & Drawing Triangles

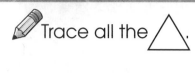 Trace all the △.

 Finish the △. Then draw a △.

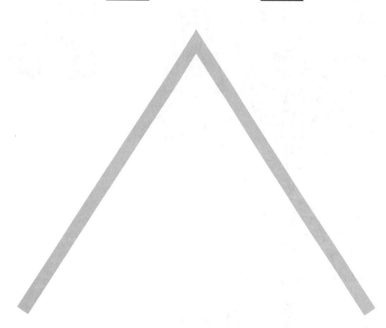

✔ all the △ in the picture.

✎ How many △ did you find? **5 6 7**

This is a **rectangle**.

✓ 2 ⬜ .

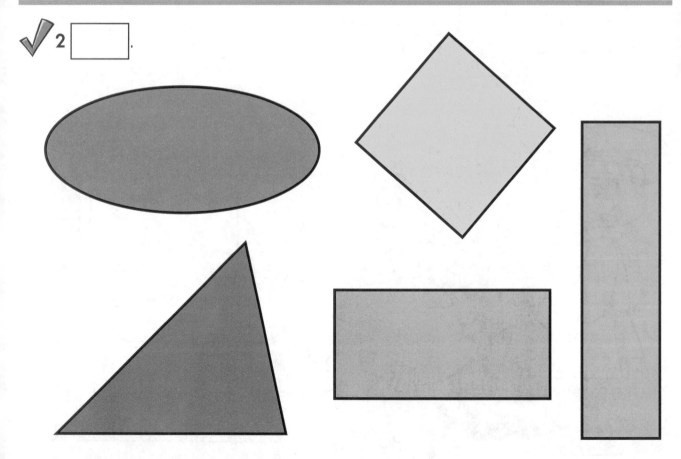

Coloring Rectangles

Color the ▢ .

Color **2** ▢ .

Color the [ ] green.

Tracing & Drawing Rectangles

✏️ Trace all the ☐.

✏️ Finish the ☐. Then draw a ☐.

Rectangle Search

✓ all the ☐ in the picture.
How many ☐ did you find? **5 6 7**

This is an **oval**.

✓2 ◯.

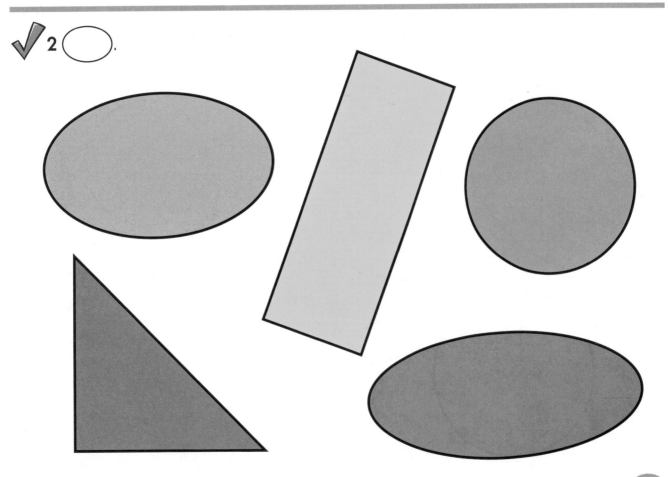

Coloring Ovals

Color the ◯.

Color 2 ◯.

 Color the ⬭ blue.

Tracing & Drawing Ovals

Trace all the 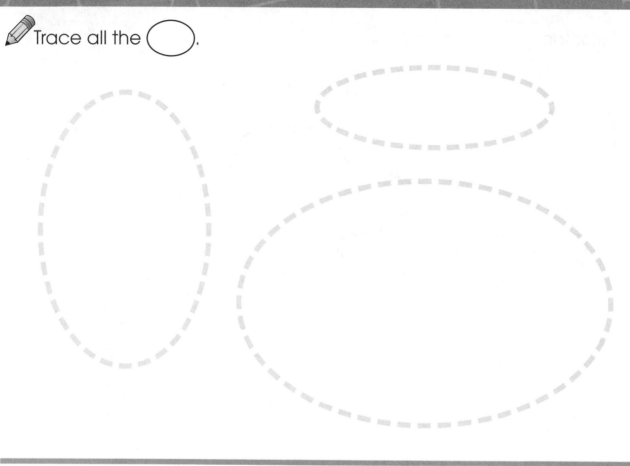.

Finish the ⬭. Then draw an ⬭.

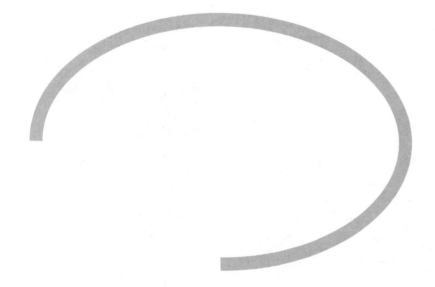

✔ all the ⬭ in the picture.

How many ⬭ did you find?   **6   7   8**

Draw lines between the shapes that **match**.

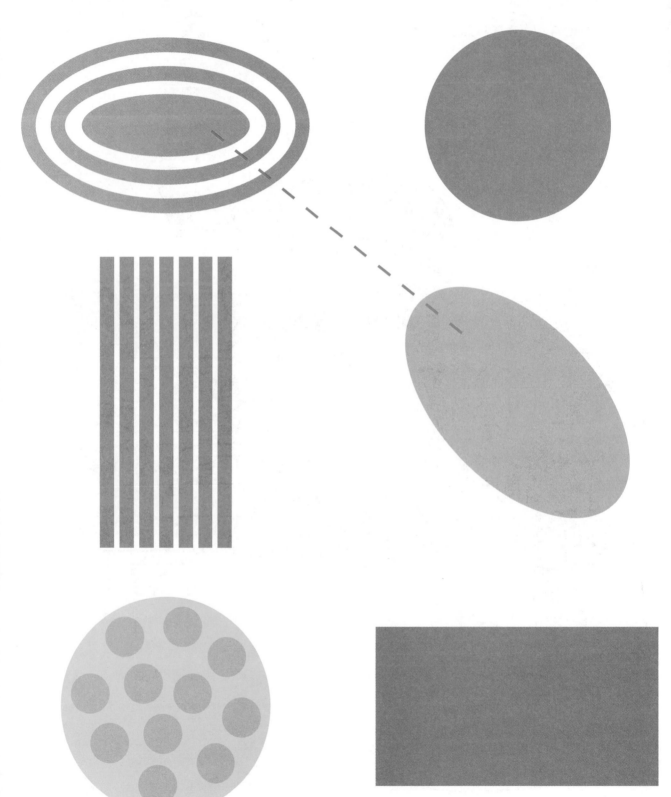

Matching Shapes

 Draw lines between the shapes that **match**.

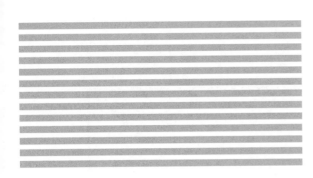

Finding & Coloring Shapes

Color all the ◯ **purple**.

Color all the ▭ **red**.

Finding & Coloring Shapes

Color all the △ yellow.

Color all the ▭ green.

 Color all the ◯ **orange**.

Color all the ▢ **blue**.

Finding & Coloring Shapes

Color all the ⬜ red.

Color all the △ green.

Color all the ◯ yellow.

Color all the ▢ blue.

Trace the ☐. Then draw a ☐.

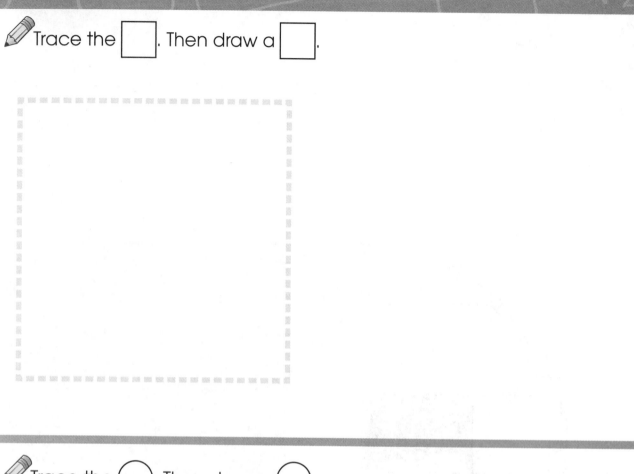

Trace the ◯. Then draw a ◯.

Tracing & Drawing Shapes

Trace the △. Then draw a △.

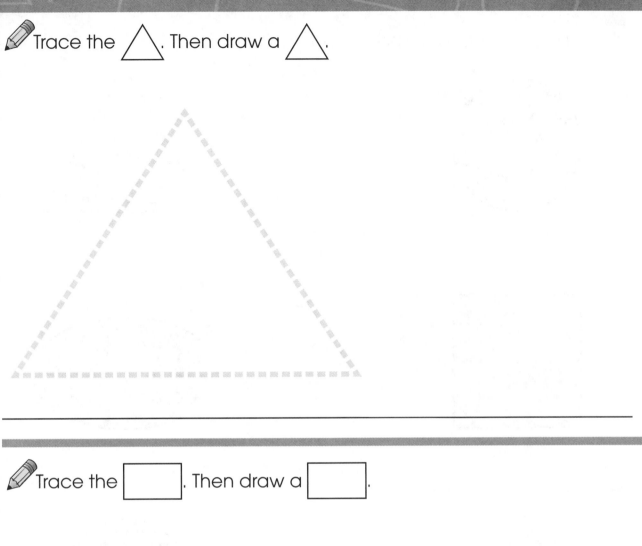

Trace the ▭. Then draw a ▭.

Matching Shapes

 Draw lines between the shapes that **match**.

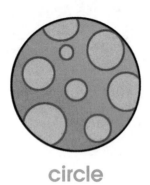

circle

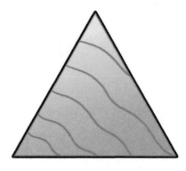

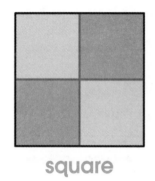

square

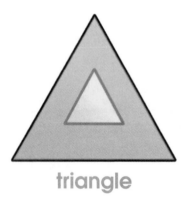

triangle

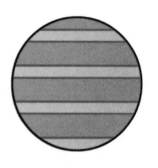

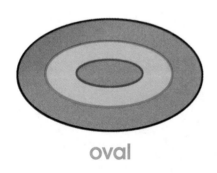

oval

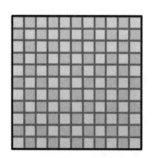

Color the picture.

▭ = pink   ◯ = blue   ◇ = purple

Color by Shape

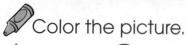 Color the picture.

△ = green   ◯ = blue   ▢ = brown

Color by Shape

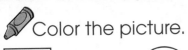 Color the picture.

☐ = orange   ⬭ = **brown**   ◇ = green

Color by Shape

Color the picture.

△ = **purple** ◯ = **brown** ▢ = **blue**

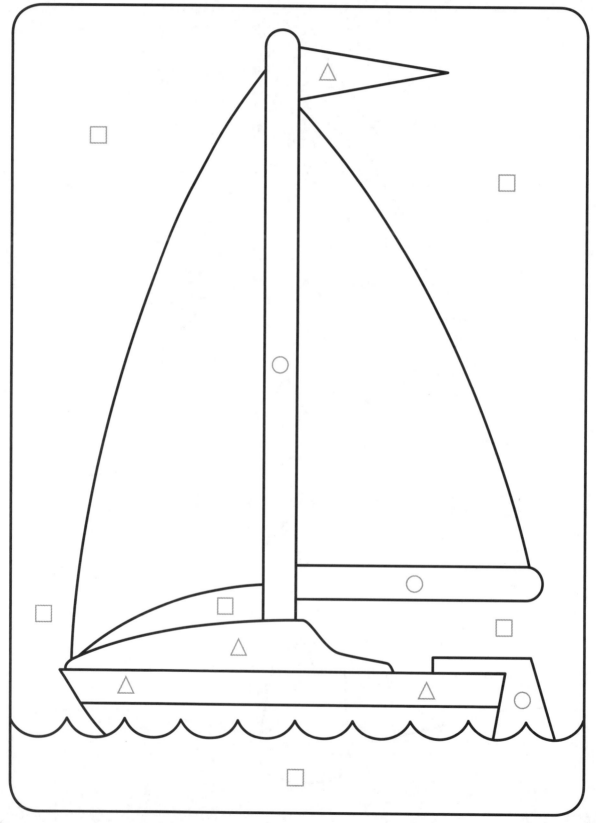

Color by Shape

Color the picture.

☐ = **purple** ◯ = green ◇ = orange

Color by Shape

Color the picture.

△ = green   ◯ = blue   ▢ = tan

Color by Shape

 Color the picture.

▭ = **green**   △ = **orange**   ◯ = **blue**   ◇ = **brown**

Color by Shape

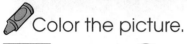 Color the picture.

⬜ = **green**   ◯ = **brown**   ⬭ = **blue**   ◇ = **gray**

Color by Shape

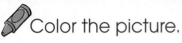Color the picture.

☐ = **brown**   △ = yellow   ○ = orange   ◇ = **blue**

Color by Shape

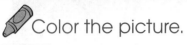 Color the picture.

□ = **blue**   △ = yellow   ◯ = **brown**   ◇ = pink

Color by Shape

 Color the picture.

△ = tan ◯ = **brown** ▢ = green ◇ = blue

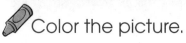Color the picture.

☐ = **blue** ◯ = pink ⬭ = **brown** ◇ = gray

Color by Shape

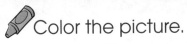 Color the picture.

△ = pink   ◯ = purple   ▢ = yellow   ◇ = blue

Shapes 49

Color by Shape

Color the picture.

☐ = **brown** △ = **red** ◯ = **purple** ☐ = **green** ◇ = **blue**

Color by Shape

Color the picture.

□ = **blue**   △ = **green**   ○ = yellow   □ = **dark green**   ○ = **blue**

1

one

⬤ **One** mouse is in the house.

✏️ Trace and write the number **1**.

🖍️ Color **1** ☆.

Finding 1

 Circle the groups of **one**.

Learning about the Number I

The Number 2

2
two

Two dogs are chasing frogs.

✏️ Trace and write the number **2**.

🖍️ Color **2** ⭐.

Circle the groups of **two**.

Fun with 1 & 2

✏️ Trace and write the numbers.

1

2 2 2

✏️ How many are there?
Write the numbers.

© School Zone Publishing Company 06343

Fun with 1 & 2

 Draw lines to match each group to the correct number.

Reviewing 1 & 2 57

3
three

●●● **Three** cats are wearing hats.

 Trace and write the number **3**.

Color **3** ☆.

Circle the groups of **four**.

Fun with 3 & 4

✏️ Trace and write the numbers.

●●● 3 3 3

●●●● 4 4 4

✏️ How many are there?
Write the numbers.

Fun with 3 & 4

 Color **4** fish **red**.

 Color **3** fish orange.

Color **2** fish **blue**.

Color **1** fish yellow.

One, Two, Three, Four

✏️ Trace the numbers. Then write the numbers.

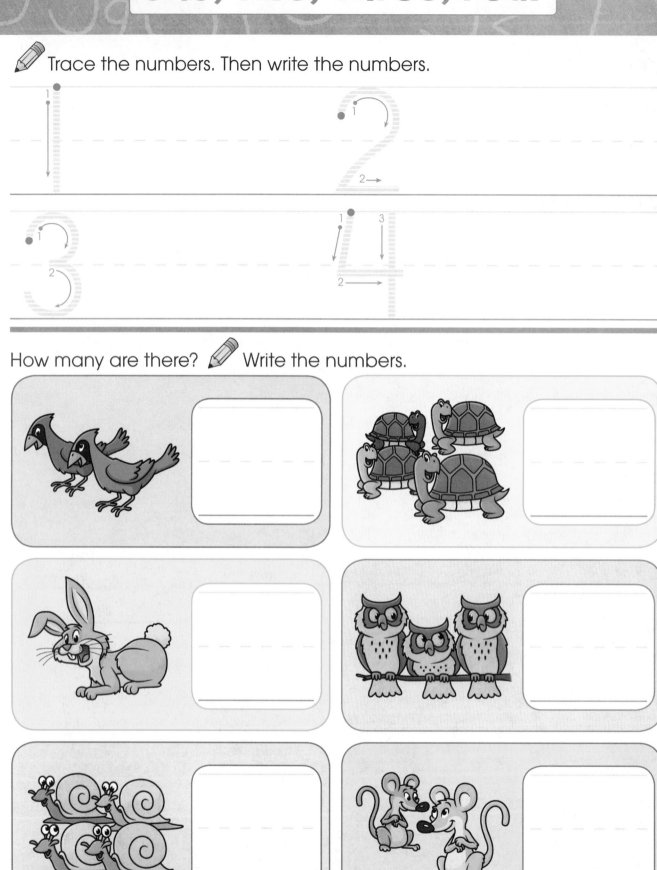

How many are there? ✏️ Write the numbers.

Which Way to the Cave?

Draw lines to help the bear get to the cave.
Use a different color to show each way.

How many ways can the bear get to the cave?   **2   3   4**

How many ways can the bear **not** get to the cave?   **2   3   4**

Counting Under the Sea

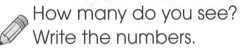 How many do you see?
Write the numbers.

© School Zone Publishing Company 06343

Color by Number

 Color the picture.

1 = pink   2 = **purple**   3 = yellow   4 = blue

5
five

●●●●● **Five** pigs are wearing wigs.

✏️ Trace and write the number **5**.

🖍️ Color **5** ⭐.

Groups of 5

✏️ Circle the groups of **five**.

6
six

Six chicks are doing tricks.

 Trace and write the number **6**.

$6\ 6\ 6$

 Color **6** ☆.

✏️ Circle the groups of **six**.

Fun with 5 & 6

✏️ Trace and write the numbers.

5 5 5

6 6 6

✏️ How many are there?
Write the numbers.

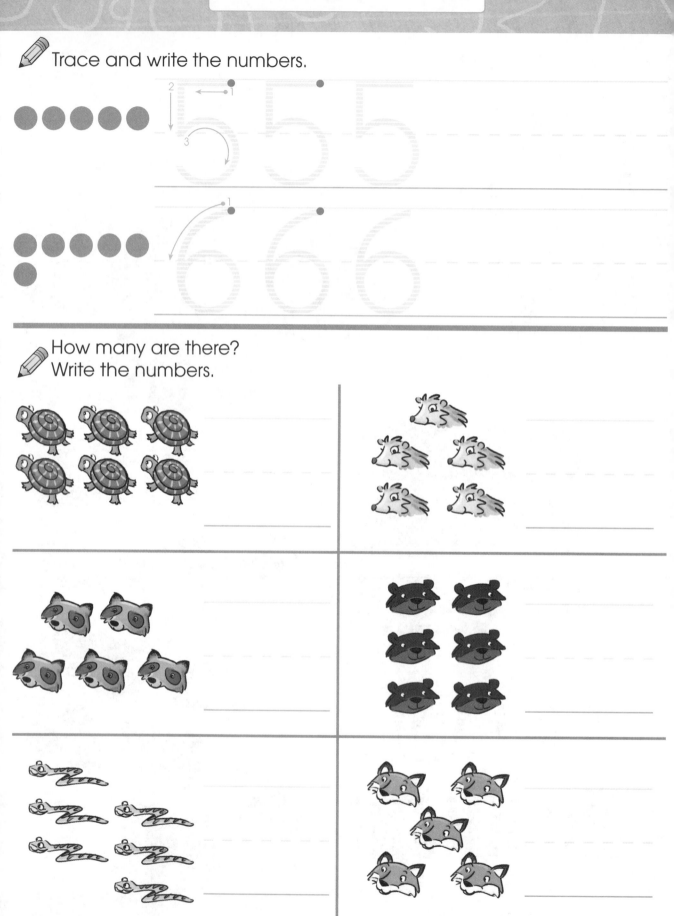

Fun with 5 & 6

Count the baby animals.
Circle how many there are of each.

4　5　6

4　5　6

4　5　6

4　5　6

4　5　6

4　5　6

7
seven

Seven sheep are in a jeep.

Trace and write the number **7**.

1 → 2

Color **7** ☆.

Circle the groups of **seven**.

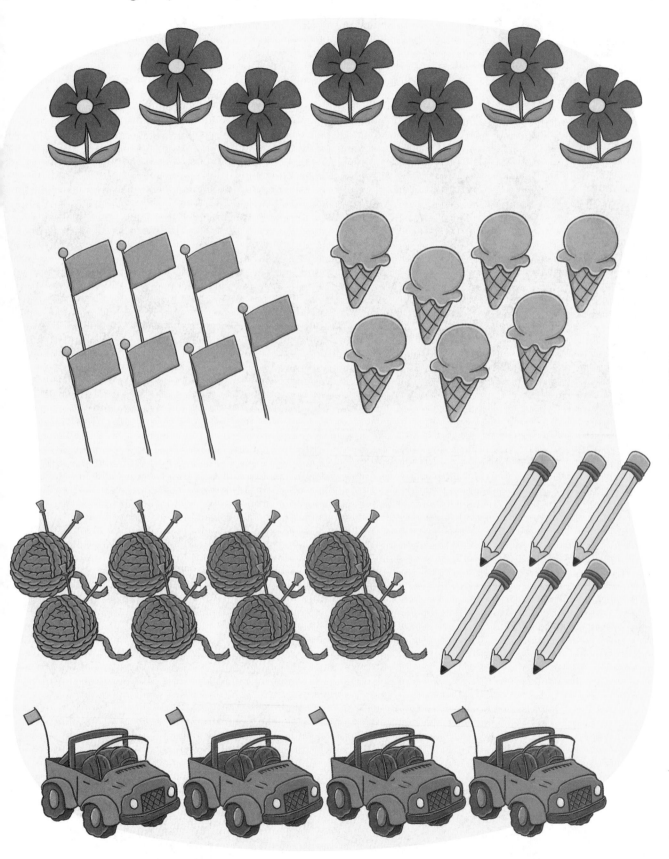

8
eight

Eight ants are wearing pants.

 Trace and write the number **8**.

 Color **8** ⭐.

Groups of 8

Circle the groups of **eight**.

Learning about the Number 8   77

Fun with 7 & 8

✏️ Trace and write the numbers.

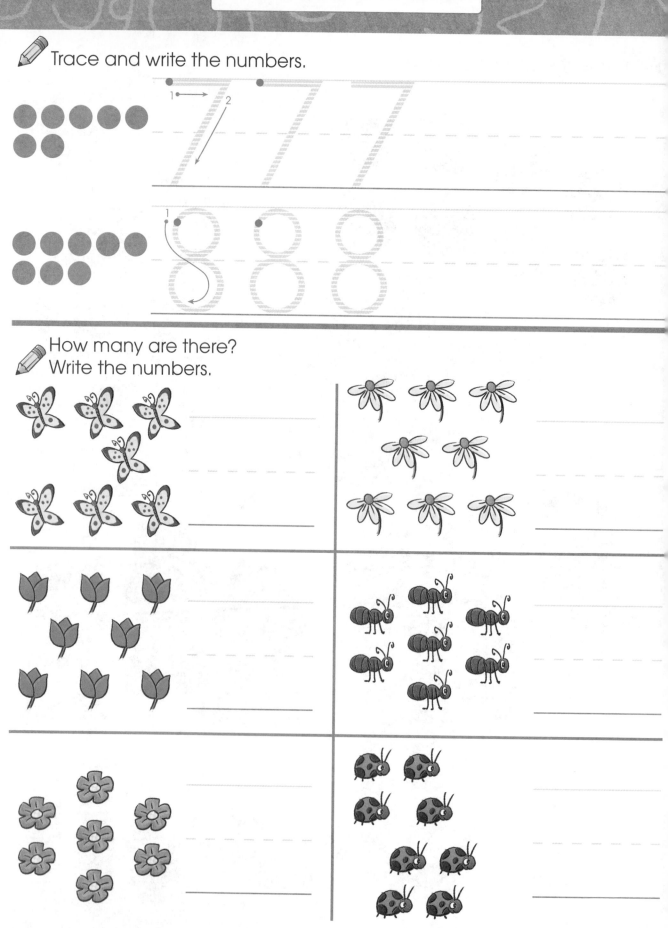

✏️ How many are there?
Write the numbers.

Fun with 7 & 8

 Count the insects and flowers.
Write how many there are of each.

✏️ Trace the numbers. Then write the numbers.

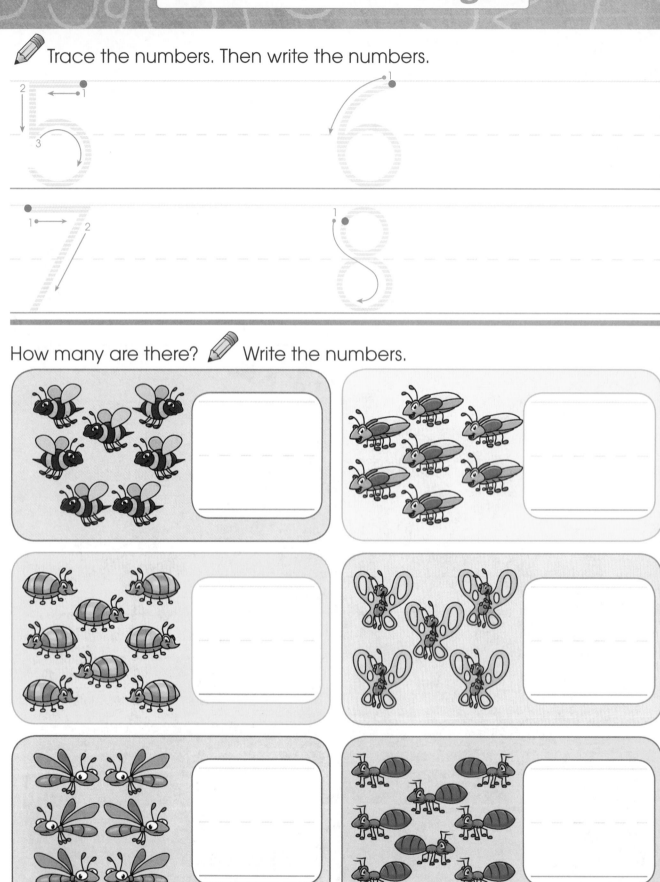

How many are there? ✏️ Write the numbers.

The Road Home

Draw a line to help each animal find its way home.

How many?　How many?　How many?

Read each number.
Color that many pieces of fruit.

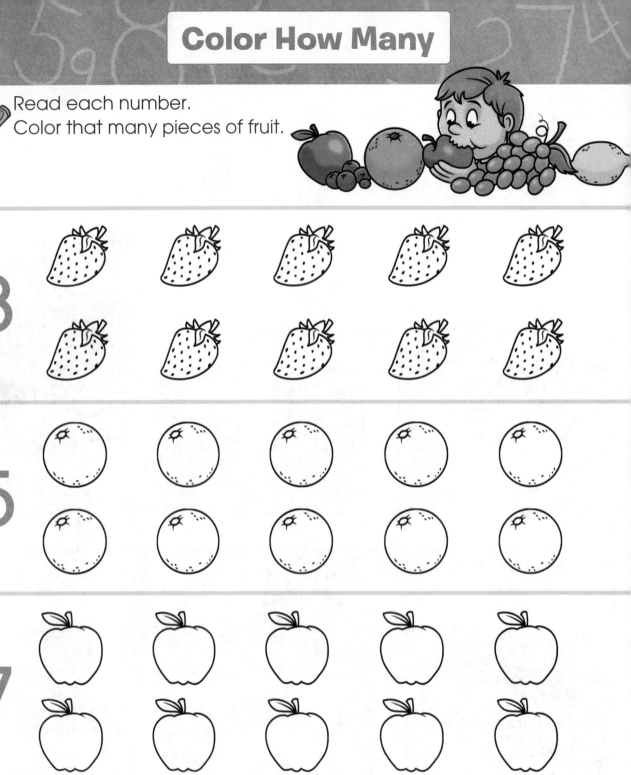

8

5

7

6

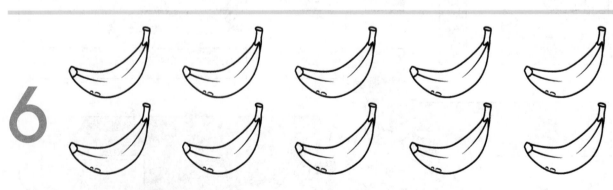

Color the picture.

5 = yellow   6 = **purple** 7 = green   8 = blue

9 nine

Nine fish are on a dish.

 Trace and write the number **9**.

 Color **9** ⭐.

Circle the groups of **nine**.

Learning about the Number 9

10
ten

Ten bees are having tea.

 Trace and write the number **10**.

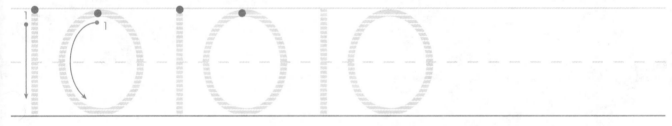

 Color **10** ☆.

© School Zone Publishing Company 06343

Circle the groups of **ten**.

✏️ Trace and write the numbers.

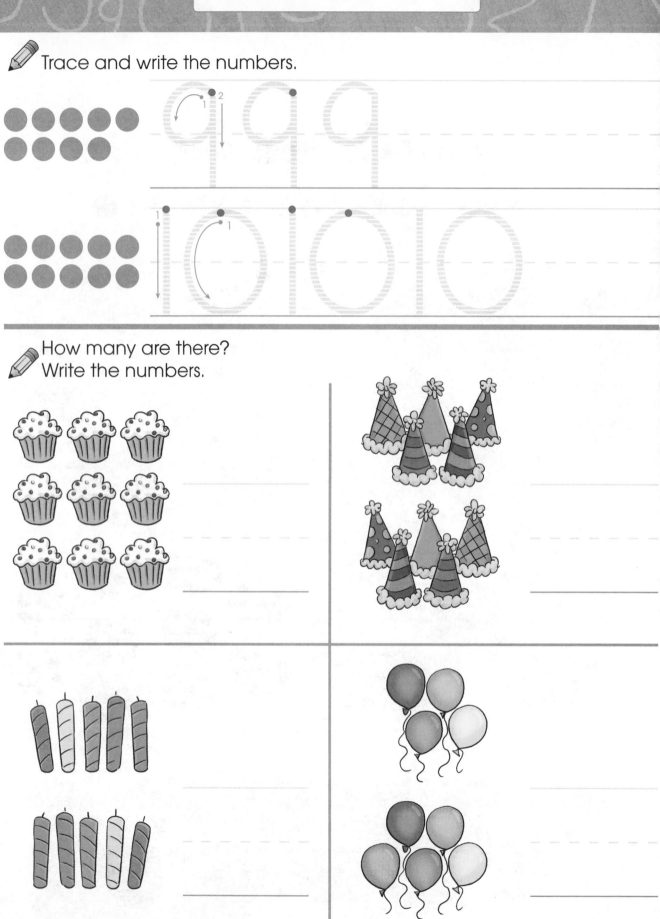

✏️ How many are there?
Write the numbers.

Fun with 9 & 10

✔ the 🐝.

✏ Circle the 🐞.

✖ the 🐜.

How many are there?

Trace the numbers. Then write the numbers.

How many are there? Write the numbers.

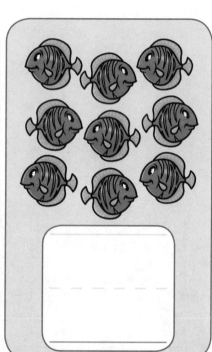

What's Missing?

Read the number in each box.
Draw the missing flowers.

8

7

10

9

Trace and write the number **0**.

 How many birds are there?
Write the numbers.

Fun with 0

✏️ Circle the nests that have **zero** birds inside.

Color the picture.

6 = **green**   7 = **red**   8 = **orange**   9 = **brown**   10 = **blue**

Color by Number

Color the picture.

1 = yellow   2 = **red**   3 = orange   4 = **green**   5 = **purple**

Circle the numbers that are the **same** as the words.

three   5   6   3   2

seven   7   8   4   1

ten   10   7   3   4

nine   10   9   2   4

A Day on the Water

✏️ Write the correct number on each line.

How many are there? _____

How many are there? 🎣 _____

How many are there? 🐟 _____

How many are there? 🦺 _____

Circle the numbers that are the **same** as the words.

 **two** 10   7   1   2

 **five** 4   12   5   8

 **four** 4   10   9   5

 **six** 12   6   7   3

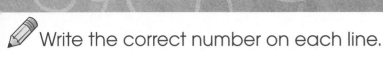

✏ Write the correct number on each line.

_____   _____

How many
are there?   _____

How many
are there?  _____

How many
are there?   _____

How many
are there?   _____

Reviewing 0 through 10   99

Circle the numbers that are the **same** as the words.

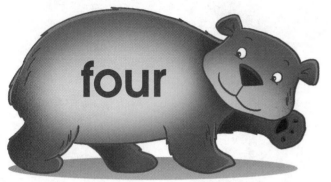

4   3   5   10

1   9   6   8

2   10   3   11

7   12   8   4

Buzzing Around

 Write the correct number on each line.

_____

 How many are there? _____

 How many are there? _____

 How many are there? _____

 How many are there? _____

Visiting the Animals

Follow the numbers from **1** to **9**.
Draw a line on the path.

The Farm

1 •

one

Circle **1** 🧑‍🌾

Circle **1** 🐔

Circle **1** 🚜

The Cow Barn

2 ••
two

✏ Circle **2** 🪣.

✏ Circle **2** 🐄.

✏ Circle **2** 🐱.

3 •••
three

✏️ Circle **3** 🐸.

✏️ Circle **3** 🐦.

✏️ Circle **3** 🐞.

4 ••••
four

✏ Circle **4** .

✏ Circle **4** 🐰.

✏ Circle **4** 🛒.

5 ●●●●●

five

🖊 Circle **5** 🦆.

🖊 Circle **5** ⊓.

🖊 Circle **5** 🐭.

FEED

6

six

✏️ Circle **6** 🍽️.

✏️ Circle **6** 🥛.

7
seven

✏️ Circle **7**

✏️ Circle **7**

8 eight

✏️ Circle **8** 🦋.

✏️ Circle **8** 🐤.

The Fairgrounds

9 ●●●●●
●●●●
nine

Circle 9 ⚑.

Circle 9 🍦.

10 ten

Circle **10** 🍭.

Circle **10** 🍩.

Circle **10** 🧁.

In the Park

✏️ Find and circle the numbers **1–10**.

An Afternoon Outside

✏️ Circle **1** hidden 🐟.

✏️ Circle **2** hidden ∿.

✏️ Circle **3** hidden ☂.

✏️ Circle **4** hidden 🐞.

Reviewing 0 through 10

Color the picture.

1 = **purple**   2 = **red**   3 = orange   4 = green   5 = blue

Color by Number

Color the picture.

6 = **yellow**   7 = **brown**   8 = **black**   9 = **red**   10 = **blue**

11
12
13
14
15
16
17
18
19
20

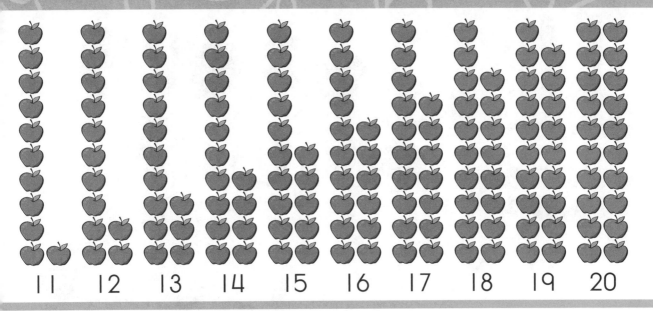

11	12	13	14	15	16	17	18	19	20

Count the apples. Circle the apples in groups of 10, then match.
The first one is done for you.

10 and More   **Number**

1.

10 and 3   11

12

2.

10 and 5   13

14

3.

10 and 2   15

16

4.

10 and 7   17

5.

10 and 10   18

19

6.

10 and 6   20

11
eleven

 Trace and write the number 11.

 Draw 11 ◯.

Color **11** 🦋.

Circle **11** 🕊.

12
twelve

✏️ Trace and write the number **12**.

✏️ Draw **12** ☐.

Circle **12** 🐟

Color **12** 🦀

13
thirteen

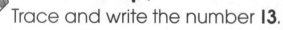
Trace and write the number 13.

Draw 13 △.

Circle **13** 🐦.

Color **13** 🦜.

© School Zone Publishing Company 06343

Learning about the Number 13 125

14
fourteen

REPTILE HOUSE

Trace and write the number 14.

Draw 14 ☐.

Reptile Roundup

SNAKES

Circle 14 🖊

Color 14 🖍

Color by Number

 Color the picture.

11 = **brown** 12 = **green** 13 = yellow 14 = **blue**

Color by Number

Color the picture.

11 = yellow 12 = red 13 = green 14 = blue

15
fifteen

✏️ Trace and write the number **15**.

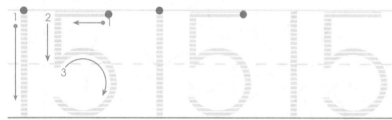

✏️ Draw **15** ◯.

Flamingo Friends

Circle **15** 🌲.

Color **15** 🦩.

Learning about the Number 15

16
sixteen

TREE HOUSE →

✏️ Trace and write the number **16**.

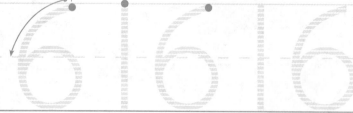

✏️ Draw **16** ◯.

Treehouse Adventure

Circle **16** 🍎.

Color **16** 🌸.

17
seventeen

✏️ Trace and write the number **17**.

17 17 17

✏️ Draw **17** ☐.

Picnic Pals

✏️ Circle **17** 🐝.

🖍️ Color **17** 🐞.

18
eighteen

Trace and write the number **18**.

Draw **18** △.

Farmyard Friends

Circle **18** 🐤

Color **18** 🐰

Color the picture.

15 = **brown**   16 = **purple**   17 = orange   18 = green

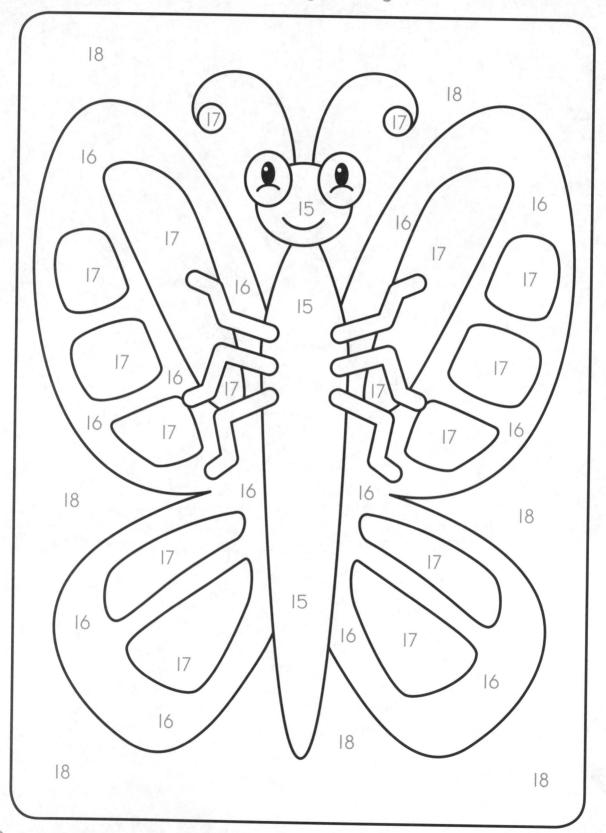

Color the picture.

15 = yellow   16 = **brown**   17 = orange   18 = **blue**

19
nineteen

✏️ Trace and write the number **19**.

✏️ Draw **19** ☐.

Gift Shop Stop

 Circle **19** .

 Color **19** .

Learning about the Number 19

20
twenty

✏️ Trace and write the number **20**.

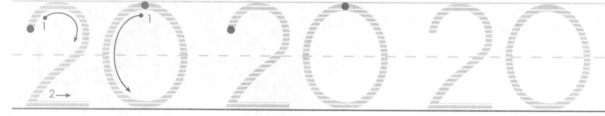

✏️ Draw **20** ◯.

Grand Garden

Circle **20** 🌸.

Color **20** 🍄.

Color the picture.

11 = pink   12 = **purple**   13 = yellow   14 = **green**   15 = **blue**

© School Zone Publishing Company 06343

Color by Number

Color the picture.

16 = **green** 17 = **orange** 18 = **red** 19 = **gray** 20 = **purple**

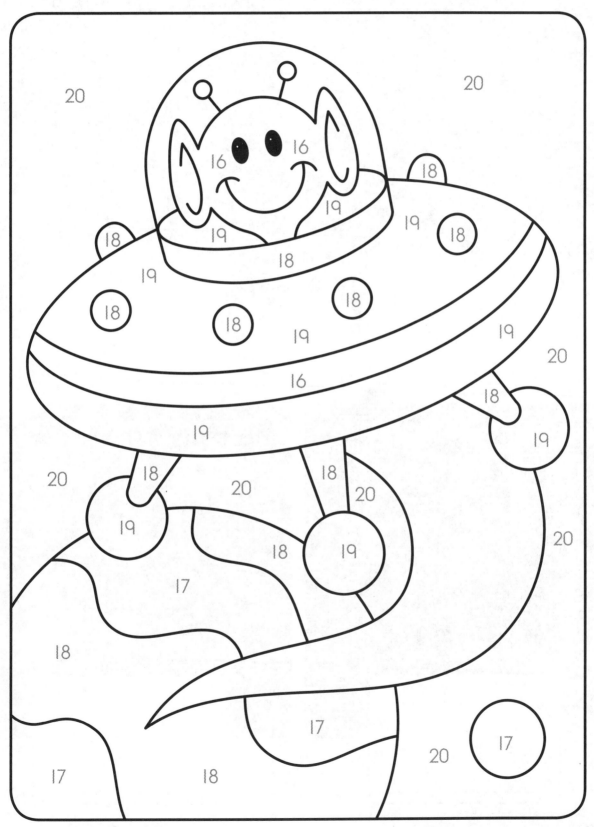

Seen on Safari

 Count the animals.
Write how many there are of each.

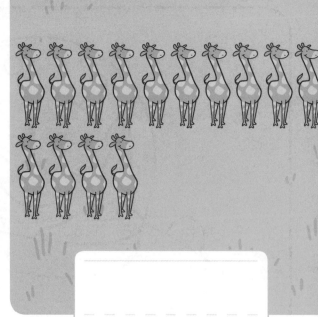

Feathered Friends

Count the birds.
Write how many there are of each.

Count the objects.
Write how many there are of each.

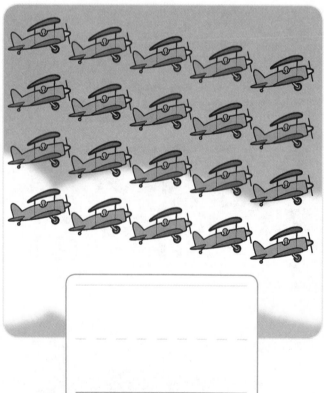

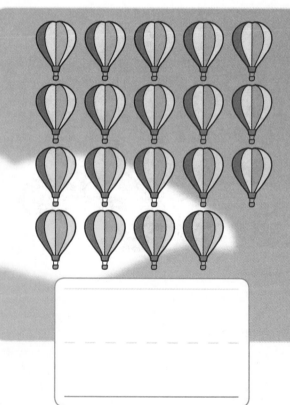

Dot-to-Dot

Connect the dots from **1** to **20**.

Color the picture and draw a 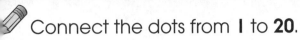 on top.

Dot-to-Dot

 Connect the dots from **1** to **20**.

 Color the picture and draw a on top.

Circle the numbers that are the **same** as the words.

twelve	2	14	12	17

fifteen	15	17	5	10

seventeen	12	10	17	7

eleven	11	8	15	6

sixteen	20	16	7	13

Circle the numbers that are the **same** as the words.

| twenty | 2 | 20 | 12 | 10 |

| fourteen | 14 | 15 | 19 | 17 |

| eighteen | 8 | 11 | 18 | 14 |

| thirteen | 14 | 12 | 13 | 19 |

| nineteen | 12 | 9 | 19 | 17 |

Circle the number that shows **how many** there are.

11	**12**	**13**

11	**12**	**13**

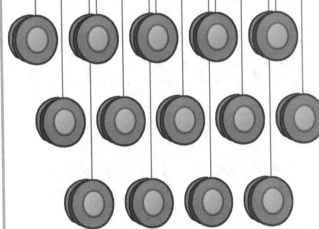

11	**12**	**13**

13	**14**	**15**

✏ Circle the number that shows **how many** there are.

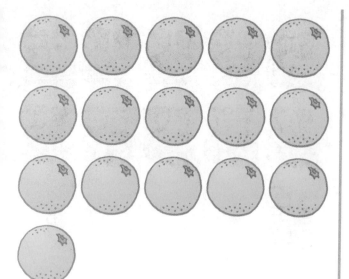

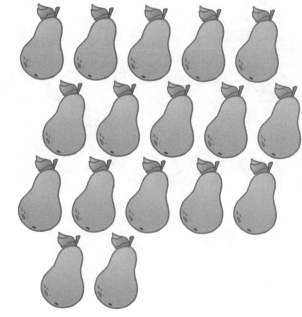

14	**15**	**16**

16	**17**	**18**

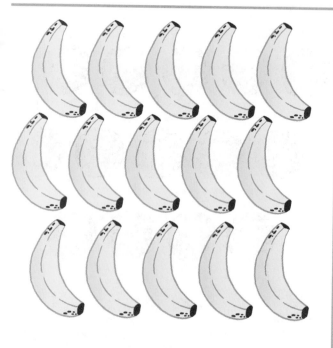

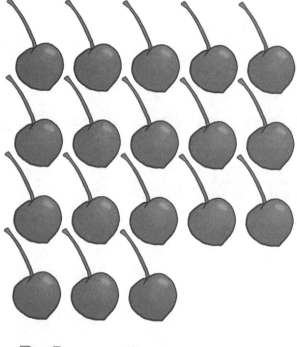

14	**15**	**16**

16	**17**	**18**

Color the picture.

11 = **yellow**   14 = **orange**   15 = **blue**

Color by Number

 Color the picture.

11 = **green**   12 = **blue**   13 = **brown**

Color by Number

 Color the picture.

13 = yellow 14 = orange 15 = blue

Color by Number

 Color the picture.

12 = **purple**   13 = **green**   14 = **red**

Color the picture.

11 = orange   14 = green   15 = blue

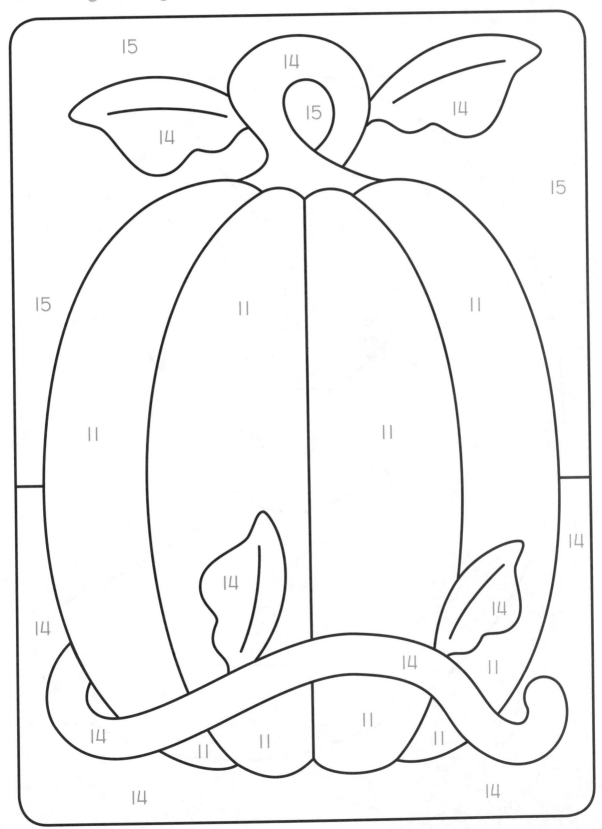

Color by Number

 Color the picture.

18 = yellow   19 = orange   20 = bue

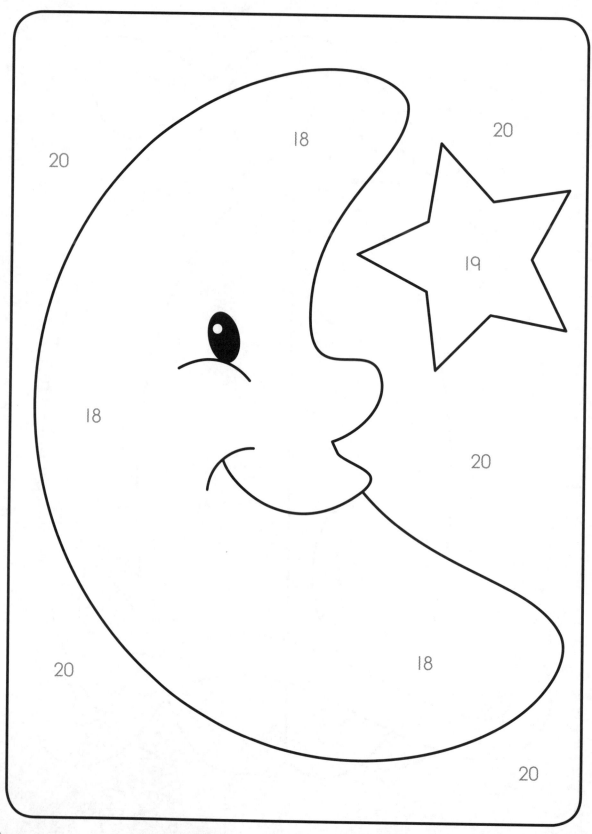

Color by Number

 Color the picture.

12 = **red** 13 = gray 14 = yellow 15 = **blue**

Color the picture.

11 = **blue**   13 = yellow   14 = **brown**   15 = orange

Color by Number

 Color the picture.

11 = yellow 12 = **purple** 14 = **brown** 15 = green

Color by Number

 Color the picture.

11 = **black** 12 = **green** 13 = **blue** 15 = **brown**

Color by Number

Color the picture.

12 = **tan**   13 = **black**   14 = **orange**   15 = **blue**

Writing Numbers

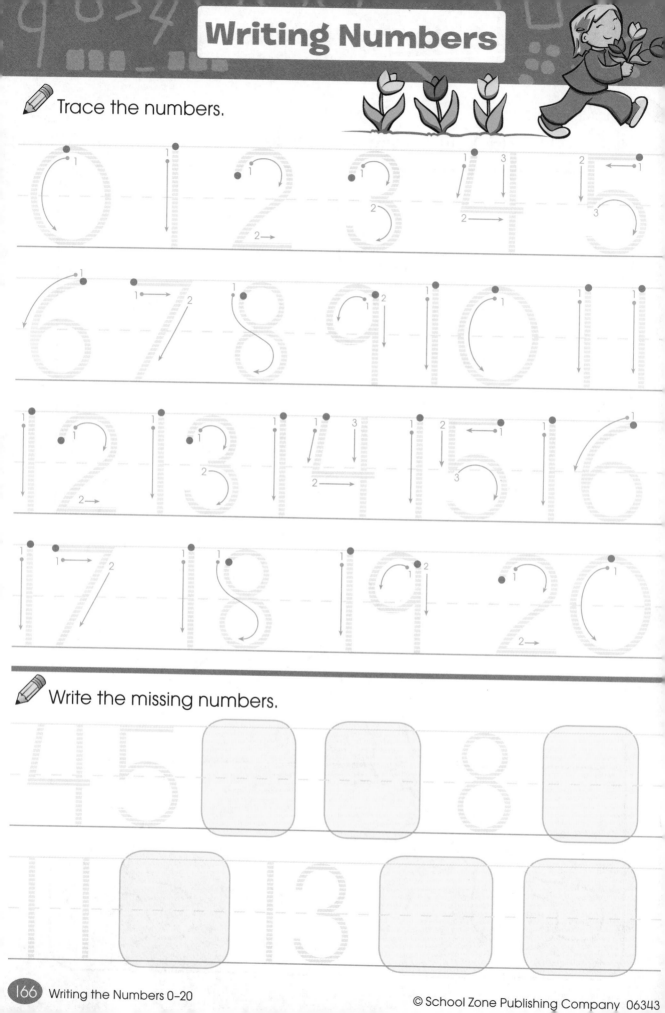

🖊 Trace the numbers.

0 1 2 3 4 5

6 7 8 9 10 11

12 13 14 15 16

17 18 19 20

🖊 Write the missing numbers.

4 5 □ □ 8 □

□ 13 □ □

Turtle Time

Connect the dots from 1 to 10.

| 1 | 2 | 3 | 4 | 5 | 6 | 7 | 8 | 9 | 10 |

Connect the dots from **11** to **20**.

Color the picture.

Up in the Sky

 Connect the dots from **1** to **20**.

 Color the picture.

Pig Pen

How many do you see?

✏️ Circle the number.

1   2   3

1   2   3

1   2   3

1   2   3

Circle how many there are.

 4 5 6

 4 5 6

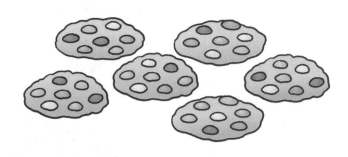 4 5 6

 4 5 6

How many vegetables or pieces of fruit are there in each group?
Draw a line from the group to the number.

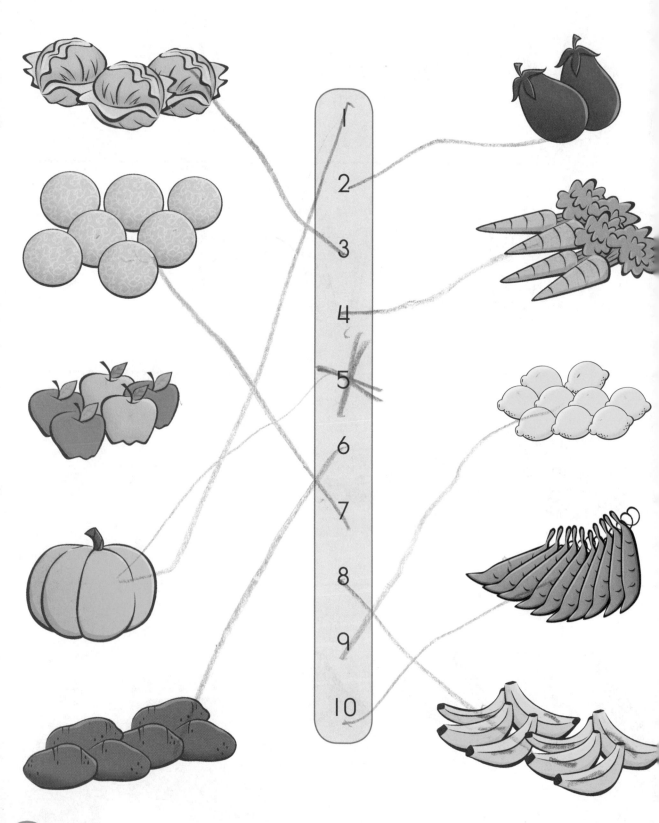

Counting on the Farm

✏️ Count the objects in the scene.
Write the correct number on each line.

Count Your Chicks

🖉 Circle the number that tells how many chicks there are in each group

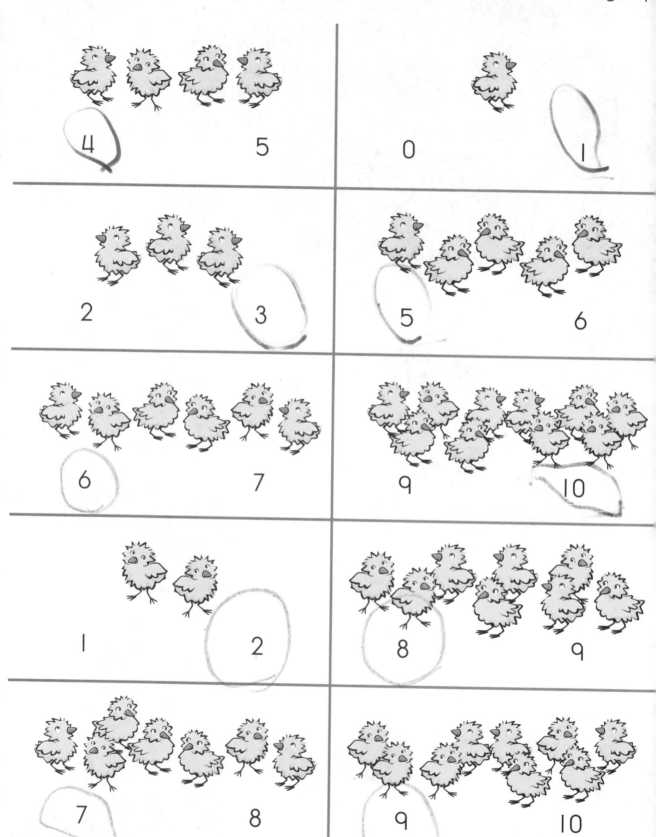

4   5

0   1

2   3

5   6

6   7

9   10

1   2

8   9

7   8

9   10

Animal Count

 Write how many animals there are in each group.

Counting Critters

✏️ Circle how many you see.

How many  are there? 6 7 **⑧**

How many 🐨 are there? **⑤** 6 7

How many 🦜 are there? 4 5 **⑥**

How many  are there?　　2　3　④

How many are there?　　5　6　⑦

How many are there?　　0　①　2

Look at All the Babies

Circle how many you see.

How many  are there?   **0   I   2**

How many  are there?   **3   4   5**

How many  are there?   **6   7   8**

How many  are there?   **5   6   7**

How many are there?   **2**   **3**   **4**

How many are there?   **5**   **6**   **7**

How many are there?   **3**   **4**   **5**

How many are there?   **1**   **2**   **3**

Color one box for each animal.
The first one is done for you.

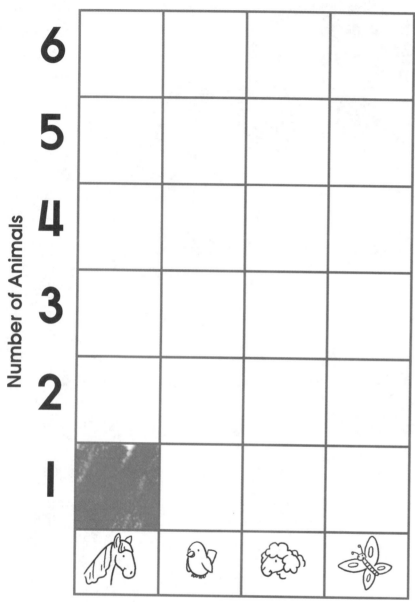

Number of Animals

6
5
4
3
2
1

Type of Animal

 Circle which animal there is the most of.

Doggy Dots

Connect the dots from **1** to **20**.
Color the picture.

Counting the Animals

Circle how many you see.

How many are there?   **4**   **5**   **6**

How many are there?   **1**   **2**   **3**

How many are there?   **6**   **7**   **8**

How many 🐑 are there?   1   2   **3**

How many 🐄 are there?   **2**   3   4

How many 🐦 are there?   5   **6**   7

How Many Legs?

Color one box for each animal.

Animals with 2 legs						
Animals with 4 legs						
	1	2	3	4	5	6

Tide Pool Count

 Circle how many you see.

How many  are there? **4** **5** **6**

How many are there? **5** **6** **7**

How many are there? **7** **8** **9**

ow many are there? 11 12 13

ow many are there? 9 10 11

ow many are there? 6 7 8

Canoe Count

✏️ Circle how many you see.

How many 🐟 are there?　**4**　**5**　**6**

How many 🛶 are there?　**1**　**2**　**3**

How many 🐸 are there?　**5**　**6**　**7**

low many  are there?   **8   9   10**

low many are there?   **7   8   9**

low many  are there?   **10   11   12**

Jungle Count

Circle how many you see on both pages.

How many 🐵 are there?   4   5   6

How many 🦎 are there?   5   6   7

How many 🐱 are there?   2   3   4

How many 🦜 are there?   7   8   9

How many 🦟 are there?   8   9   10

Color one box for each animal or insect you see on both pages.

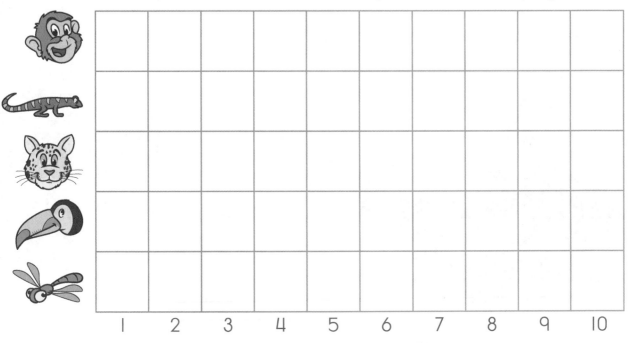

| | 1 | 2 | 3 | 4 | 5 | 6 | 7 | 8 | 9 | 10 |

Circle which animal there is the most of.

Apple Trees

Draw 🍎 on the tree.

Draw as many 🍎 as you want.

Write how many 🍎.

Draw lines from the sets of sheep to the correct pens.

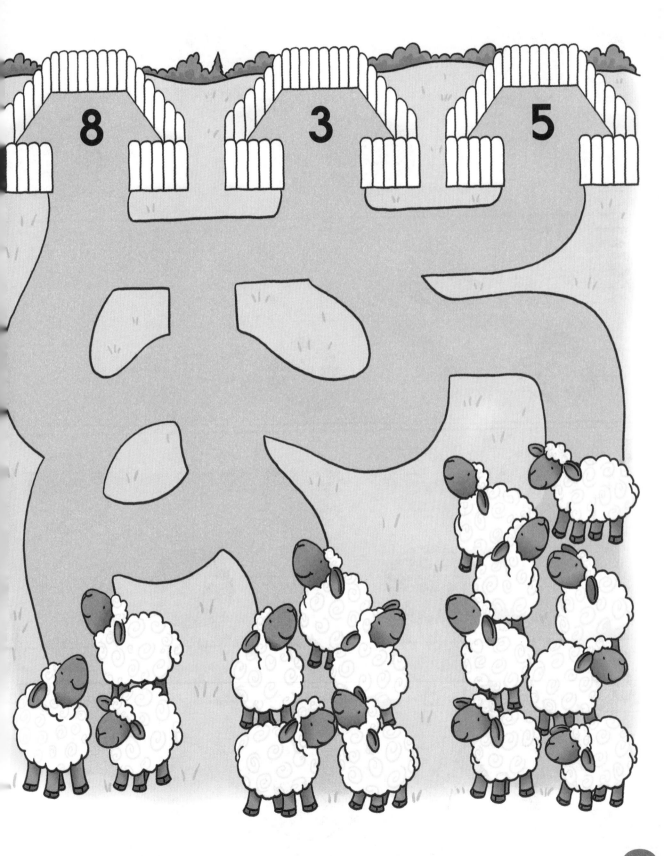

Read the numbers.
Draw the missing pieces of fruit.

8

5

II

6

Write the numbers that come **before**.

2 3

5 6

4 5

9 10

10 11

6 7

3 4

8 9

7 8

11 12

Between

2 comes **between** 1 and **3**.

1 2 3

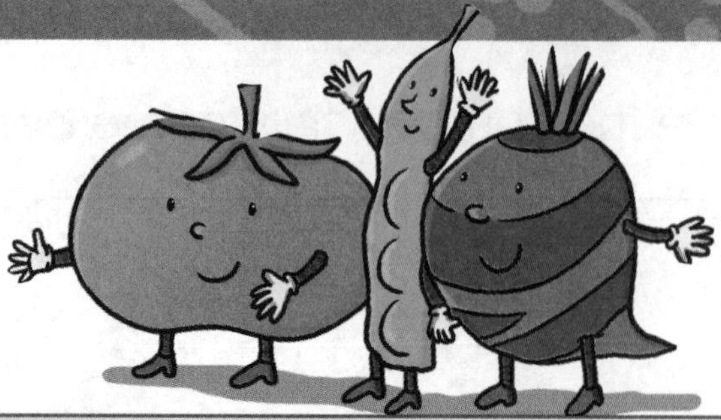

1 2 3 4 5 6 7 8 9 10 11 12 13 14 15 16 17 18 19 20

What comes **between**?
Write the correct number on each line.

3 ____ 5	2 ____ 4
6 ____ 8	5 ____ 7
4 ____ 6	8 ____ 10
7 ____ 9	1 ____ 3

Which Group Has More?

 ← This group has **more** slices of pie.

✏️ Circle the group that has **more** pieces of fruit.

  |

  |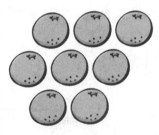

  |

 Draw a group of to show **2 more** than **3**.

How many did you draw? _____

Greater means **more than**.

⑧is **greater than 7**.

 Write how many are in each group.
Circle the number that is **greater**.

✏️ Draw a set of ⭐ to show **1 more than 3**.

How many ⭐ are there? _____

Write how many there are in each group.
Circle the **greater** number.

_____   _____

_____   _____

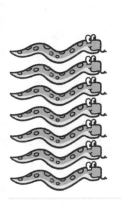 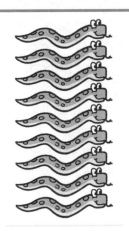    

_____   _____

_____   _____

Circle the number that is **greater**.

7 3   6 10   8 4

Concept of Greater **211**

5 horses

3 horses

5 is **greater** than **3**.

 Write how many there are in each group.
Circle the **greater** number.

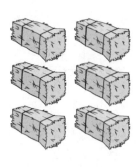

Circle the group that has a **greater** number.

2

3

9

6

8

7

6

8

One More

 is **one more** than .

✏️ Circle the group that has **one more** than the first one.

Concept of More

Circle the group that has **one more** than the first one.

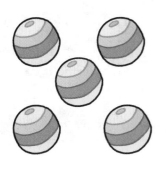 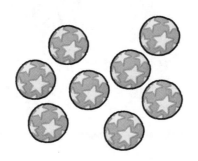 

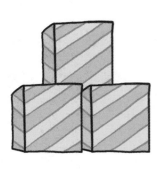 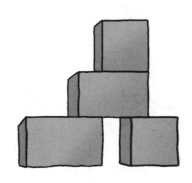 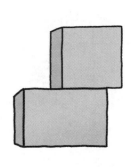

Which Number Is Less?

(8) flowers

9 flowers

8 is **less** than 9.
Less means **fewer** or **not as many**.

✏️✏️ Write how many there are in each group.
Circle the number that is **less**.

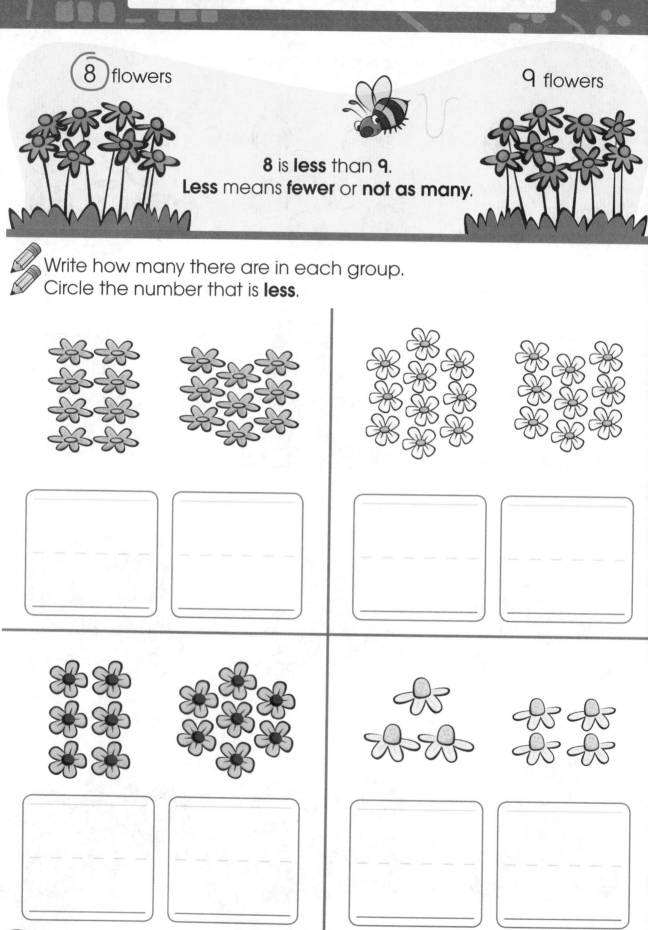

ess means **not as many.**

 ⑦ is **less than 8.**

Write how many are in each group.
Circle the number that is **less.**

Draw a set of ♥ to show **1 less than 3.**

How many ♥ are there? _____

Concept of Less   217

Write how many there are in each group.
Circle the number that is **less**.

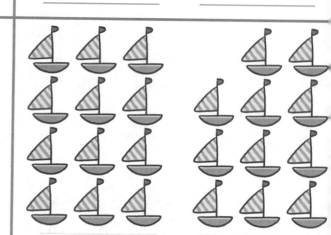

 Circle the number that is **less**.

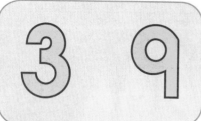 3 9

 4 5

 10 6

© School Zone Publishing Company 06343

This group has **fewer** books.

 Circle the group in each row that has **fewer**.

 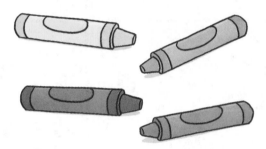

One Fewer

 is **one fewer** than .

 Circle the group that has **one fewer** than the first one.

One Fewer

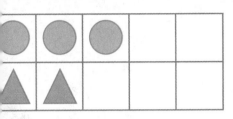

Circle how many you see.

 How many are there?　　2　③　4

How many ▲ are there?　　②　3　4

✏️ Draw 🥕 to show **one fewer** 🥕 than 🐰.

✏️ Circle how many you see.

How many 🐰 are there?　　**4**　**5**　**6**

How many 🥕 are there?　　**4**　**5**　**6**

✏️ Draw 🥚 to show **one fewer** 🥚 than 🐦.

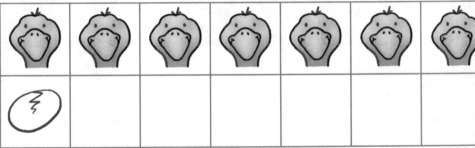

✏️ Circle how many you see.

How many 🐦 are there?　　**5**　**6**　**7**

How many 🥚 are there?　　**5**　**6**　**7**

Fewer Food Groups

 Circle the group that has **one fewer** than the first one.

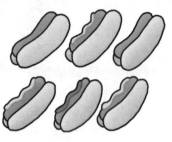 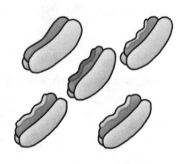 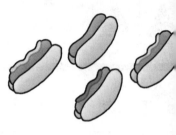

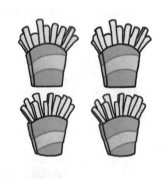  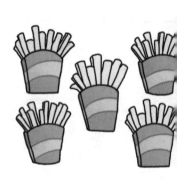

Fewer Animals

Circle the group that has **fewer**.

3

4

2

6

5

8

7

9

4

9

3

7

Lemonade Stand

How many are there?
Guess. Then count.

	🐦	🍋	🥕
Guess			
Count			

© School Zone Publishing Company 063

How many are there?
Guess. Then count.

	🌼	🥤	🐞
Guess			
Count			

Use the graph to answer the questions.

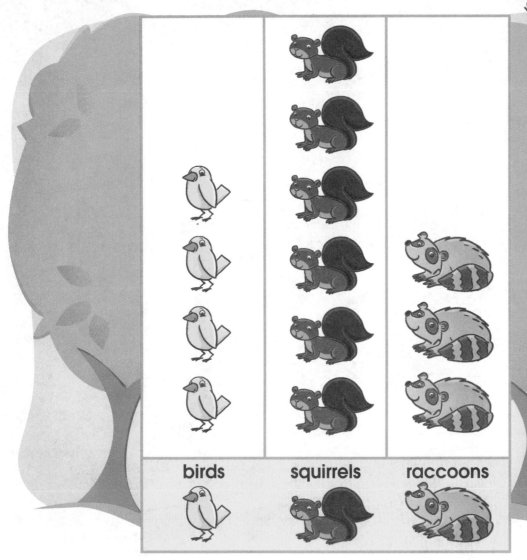

| birds | squirrels | raccoons |

 How many are there?
Write the numbers.

Are there more than ?   **Yes**   **No**

Color the graph to show how many
fruits and vegetables are at the farm stand.

1	2	3	4	5

Missing Number Mystery

Write the missing numbers in the blanks.

1 2 3 4 5 6 7 8 9 10 11 12 13 14 15 16 17 18 19 20

14 15 ___ ___ 18

___ 17 18 19 ___

11 ___ 13 14 ___

___ 14 15 ___ 17

10 11 ___ 13 ___

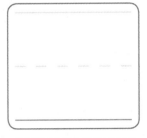

Write the numbers that come **before**.

 13

  14

18

17

19

  20

 15

  16

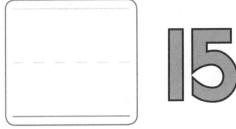 11

  12

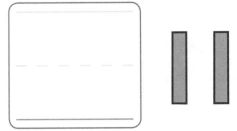

Concept of Before 229

What Comes Before?

✏️ Write the numbers that come **before**.

13   14   15

18   19   20

15   16   17

11   12   13

✏️ Write the numbers that come **between**.

12 [____] 14   11 [____] 13

13 [____] 15   10 [____] 12

9 [____] 11   15 [____] 17

18 [____] 20   8 [____] 10

Running After

✏️ Write the numbers that come **after**.

13

14

18

17

19

10

15

16

11

12

What Comes After?

Write the numbers that come **after**.

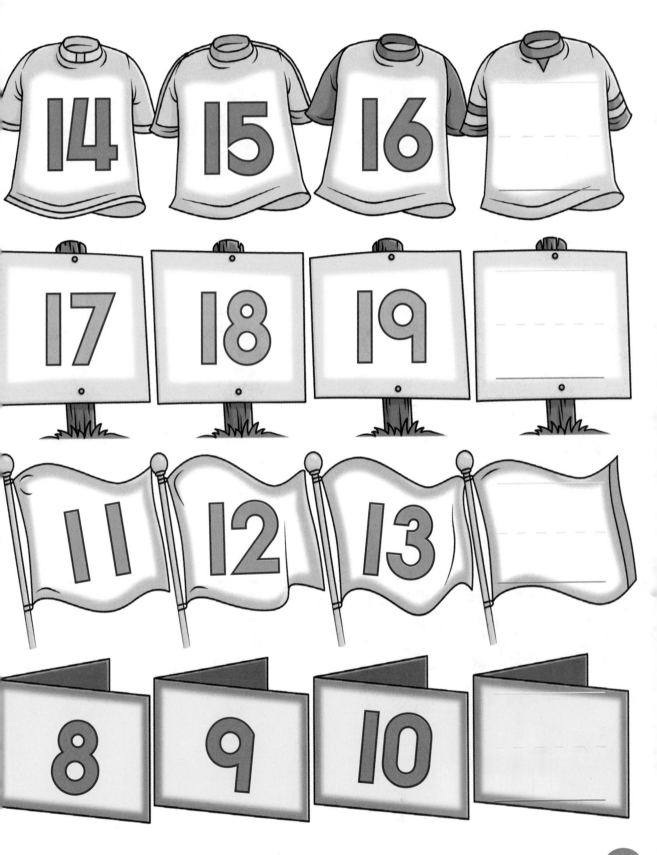

© School Zone Publishing Company 06343

More Fish

Which tank has **more** fish?
Count the fish in each tank.
Write the number.
Circle the tank that has **more** fish.

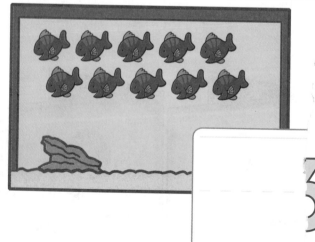

Fun with Flowers

Count how many flowers there are in each box.
Write how many there are **in all**.

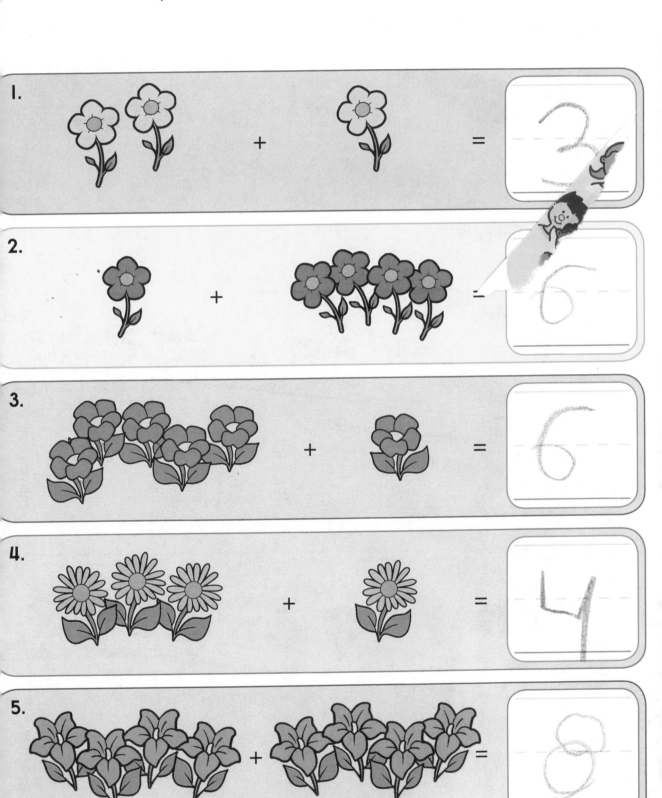

1. $+$ $=$ 3

2. $+$ $=$ 6

3. $+$ $=$ 6

4. $+$ $=$ 4

5. $+$ $=$ 8

Racing Riders

 Help count the people on each ride.
Fill in the missing number to finish the addition sentence.

1.

 + =

2 + 1 = 3

2.

 +  =

1 + 3 = 4

3.

 + =

2 + 2 = 4

Awesome Audience

Help count the people on each ride.
Fill in the missing number to finish the addition sentence.

1.

1 $+$ 4 $=$ 

2.

2 $+$ 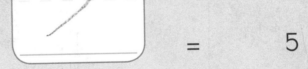 $=$ 5

3.

 $+$ 2 $=$ 6

Adding Flowers

 How many are there in all?
Write the **sum**.

$1 + 1 = 2$

1.

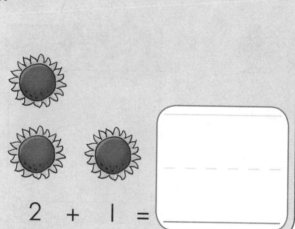

$2 + 1 = $ _____

2.

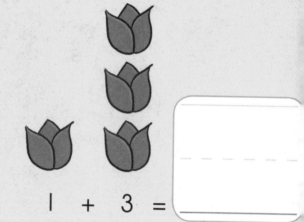

$1 + 3 = $ _____

3.

$3 + 1 = $ _____

4.

$2 + 2 = $ _____

5.

$2 + 3 = $ _____

6.

$3 + 2 = $ _____

How many are left?
Write the **difference**.

Subtracting shows how many are **left**.

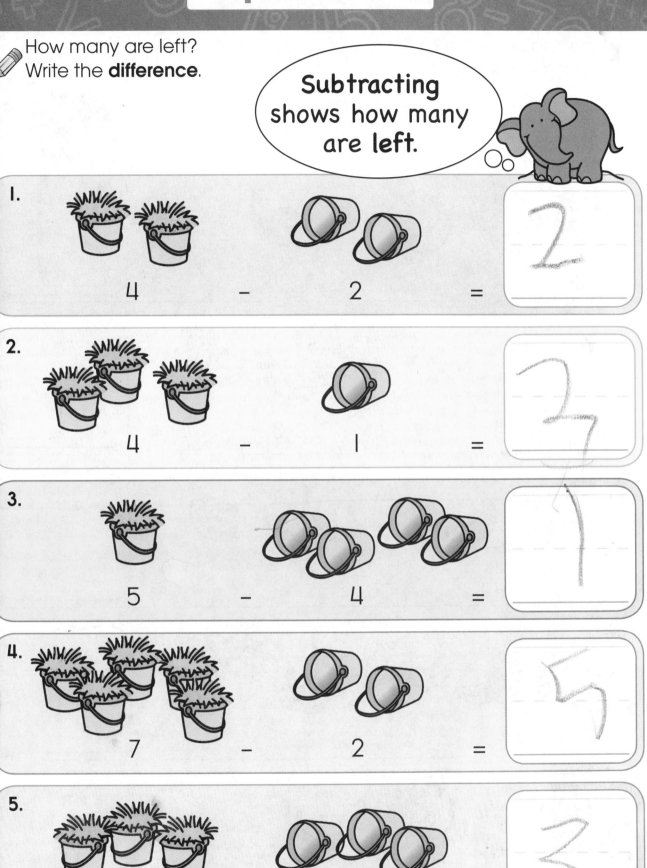

1. 4 – 2 = 2

2. 4 – 1 = 3

3. 5 – 4 = 1

4. 7 – 2 = 5

5. 6 – 3 = 3

Going Bananas

 How many are left?
Write the **difference**.

1.

5 − 1 = 4

2.

4 − 3 = 1

3.

5 − 3 = 2

4.

8 − 4 = 4

5.

7 − 2 = 5

Shopping with Pennies

Count the pennies and find the items that cost those amounts.
Draw a line from the pennies to the item that costs that much.

How Many Pennies?

 Read the amounts on the price tags.
Color that many pennies orange.

 11¢

 9¢

 12¢

 10¢

How Many Pennies?

Read the amounts on the price tags.
Color that many pennies orange.

 10¢

 6¢

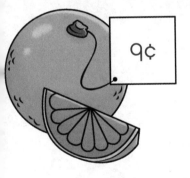 9¢

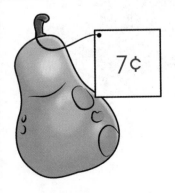 7¢

More Money

Which piggy bank has more money in it?

 ✓ the piggy bank that has **more** money.

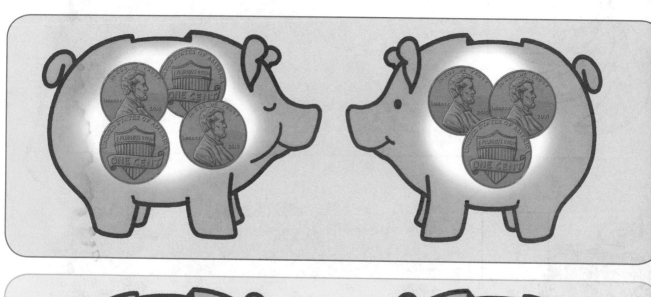

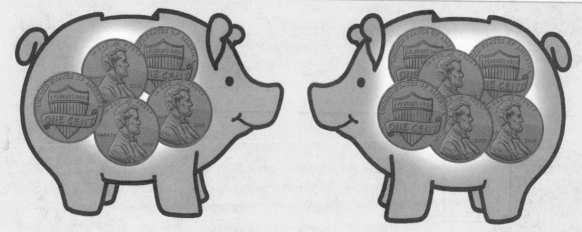

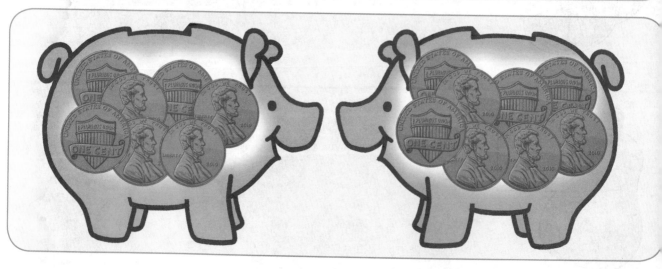

© School Zone Publishing Company 06302

Which purse has less money in it?

✓ the purse that has **less** money.

Concept of Less Money 275

Nice Nickels

The **nickel**

front   **back**

1 nickel = 5¢

How many cents are there?
Write the number.

1.

2.

 ¢

3.

 ¢

4.

 ¢

How Many Nickels and Pennies?

Read the amounts on the price tags.
Color the nickels gray and the pennies orange to make the amounts.
Use the fewest number of coins needed.

Telling Time

✏️ Write the missing numbers on the clock.
🖍️ Color the minute hand **blue**.
🖍️ Color the hour hand **red**.

When the minute hand points to the 12, we say 'clock. The hour hand pointing to the 3. It is o'clock.

3:00

 Write the times below the clocks.

_____

_____

_____

_____

Write the times below the clocks.

_____

_____

_____

_____

_____

_____

_____

_____

Telling Time

Draw hands on the clock faces.
Write the times on the digital clocks.
The first one is done for you.

I. 5 o'clock

2. 10 o'clock

3. 6 o'clock

4. 12 o'clock

5. 3 o'clock

6. 8 o'clock

✏️ Look at the times written below the clocks. Draw the hour hand on the clocks to make the clocks show those times.

2:00

4:00

7:00

8:00

Clock Repair Shop

The clocks in the repair shop are all mixed up.
How many clocks are showing each time?
Write how many clocks are telling the same time.

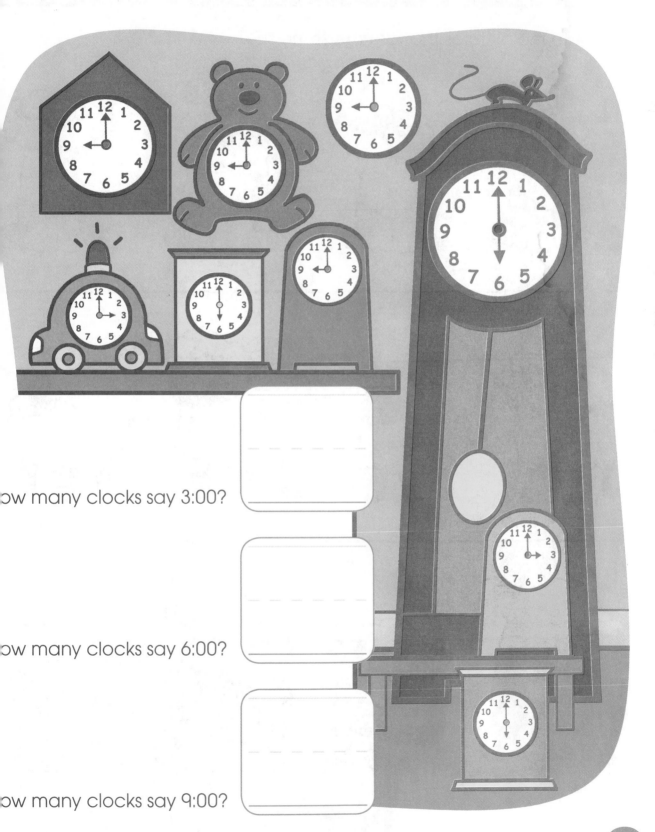

ow many clocks say 3:00?

ow many clocks say 6:00?

ow many clocks say 9:00?

These  are the **same** size.

 Circle the pictures that are the **same** size.

Garden Giants

 his is big.   This is small.

Circle the picture that is **bigger** in each row.

Pond Friends

 Circle the picture that is **bigger** than the first one.

Trouble in the Henhouse

Circle the picture that is **smaller** than the first one.

Shoo, Crows!

Use a  to measure each scarecrow.

✏️ Write how many tall is each one is.

1.

2.

3.

What Comes Next?

Color the picture to continue the pattern.

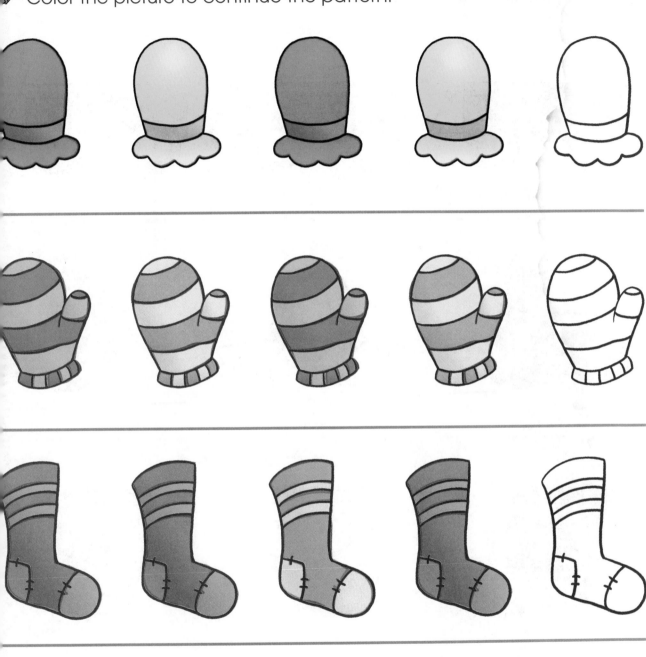

What Comes Next?

 Color the picture to continue the pattern.

What Comes Next?

 Circle the correct picture to continue the pattern.

 Circle the correct picture to continue the pattern.

 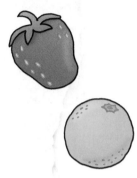

Color by Number

 Color the picture.

0 = **blue**   10 = yellow   20 = **purple**

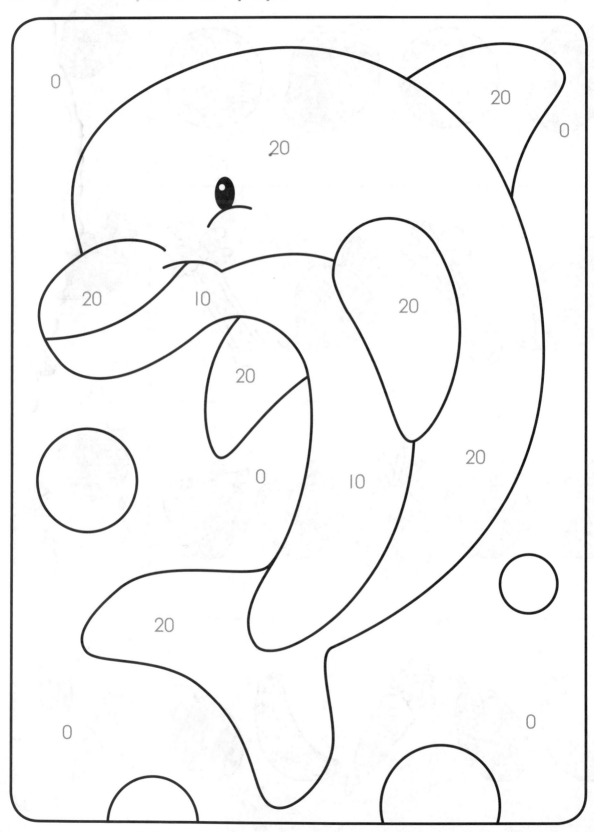

Color by Number

 Color the picture.

13 = green 2 = orange 7 = brown

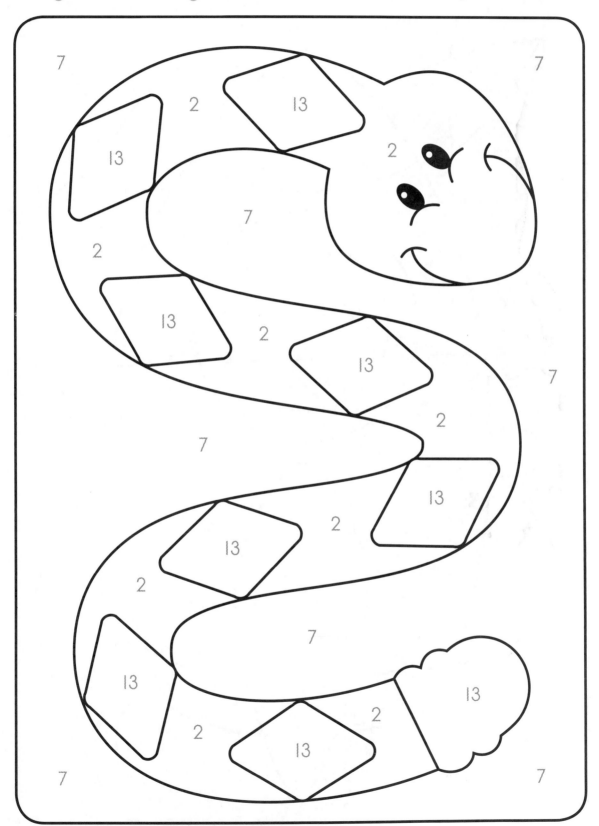

Color by Number

 Color the picture.

16 = **red** 17 = **gray** 18 = **blue**

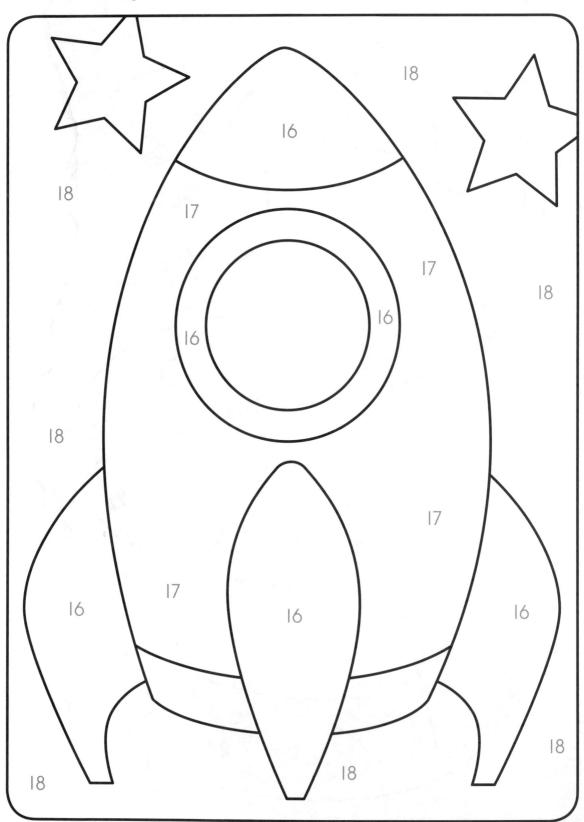

Color by Number

Color the picture.

8 = **blue**   9 = **purple**   10 = orange

Color by Number

 Color the picture.

1 = **brown**   2 = yellow   3 = **black**

Color by Number

Color the picture.

18 = **blue**   19 = **brown**   20 = **green**

Color by Number

 Color the picture.

4 = **blue** 5 = **pink** 6 = **green**

Number Maze

Draw a line through the maze to get from **0** to **20**.

Finding Addition

 Read the addition sentences.

 Write the **sums**.

 Find and circle the addition sentences in the puzzle.
The first one is done for you.

$1 + 1 = \underline{2}$ $4 + 4 = \underline{}$ $7 + 2 = \underline{}$ $5 + 1 = \underline{}$

$2 + 1 = \underline{}$ $2 + 6 = \underline{}$ $2 + 3 = \underline{}$ $7 + 0 = \underline{}$

$2 + 2 = \underline{}$ $1 + 8 = \underline{}$ $4 + 1 = \underline{}$ $4 + 3 = \underline{}$

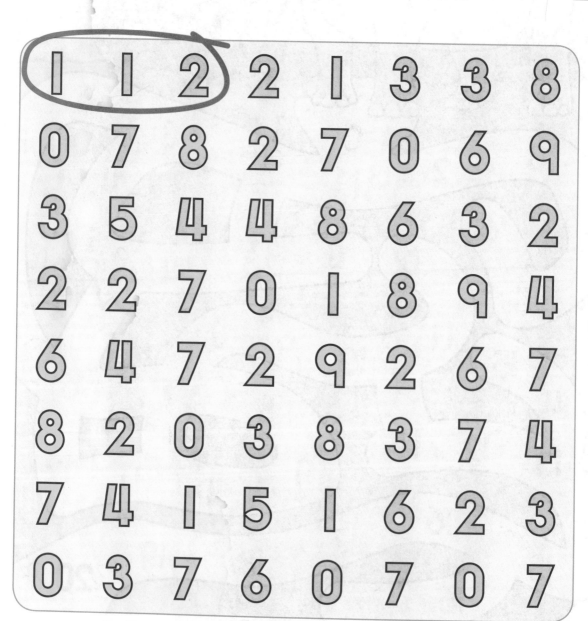

Finding Addition

Read the addition sentences.
Write the **sums**.
Find and circle the addition sentences in the puzzle.

10 + 9 = ____   2 + 8 = ____   13 + 2 = ____

5 + 8 = ____   7 + 7 = ____   2 + 12 = ____

5 + 5 = ____   8 + 6 = ____   12 + 8 = ____

16 + 2 = ____   9 + 11 = ____   10 + 4 = ____

6	10	9	19	17	2	16	7
2	0	20	1	6	19	14	10
10	7	4	5	8	13	0	4
14	16	12	5	1	2	12	14
9	2	8	10	19	15	8	19
20	18	6	3	9	11	20	6
7	7	14	18	4	0	7	14
4	16	0	6	19	8	12	9

Read the subtraction sentences.
Write the **differences**.
Find and circle the subtraction sentences in the puzzle.
The first one is done for you.

2 – 1 = __1__   8 – 6 = ____   8 – 4 = ____   3 – 0 = ____

8 – 1 = ____   6 – 2 = ____   9 – 9 = ____   9 – 4 = ____

8 – 5 = ____   4 – 1 = ____   9 – 2 = ____   6 – 5 = ____

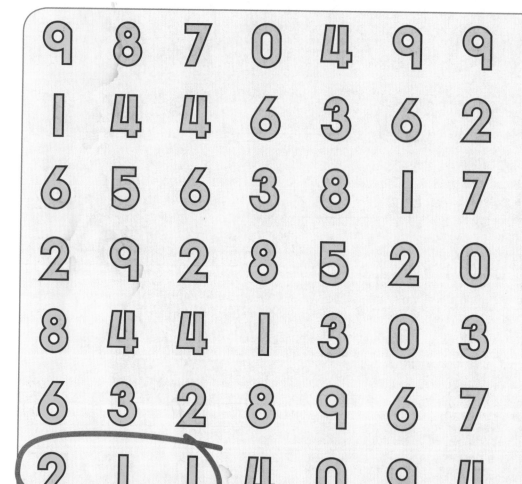

Subtraction Search

Read the subtraction sentences.
Write the **differences**.
Find and circle the subtraction sentences in the puzzle.

11 – 4 = _____   20 – 9 = _____   19 – 18 = _____

18 – 2 = _____   16 – 3 = _____   20 – 6 = _____

16 – 1 = _____   18 – 5 = _____   19 – 6 = _____

15 – 3 = _____   14 – 2 = _____   19 – 10 = _____

4	20	12	9	19	16	1	15
3	18	2	16	4	2	12	3
16	3	13	17	18	20	0	12
17	8	15	19	10	9	17	13
2	19	7	6	3	11	4	7
14	18	5	13	0	17	20	16
17	1	16	2	15	8	3	19
9	20	15	20	6	14	2	12

Answer Key

There is no answer key for pages 1–113, 118, 120–145, 155–165, and 294–303.

Page 114

Page 115

Page 116

Page 117

Page 119

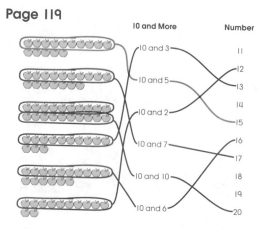

Page 146

11, 14
12, 13

Page 147

16, 15
18, 17

Page 148

18, 20
20, 19

Page 149

Page 150

Page 151

twelve	2	14	(12)	17
fifteen	(15)	17	5	10
seventeen	12	10	(17)	7
eleven	(11)	8	15	6
sixteen	20	(16)	7	13

Answer Key

Page 152

enty	2	(20)	12	10
urteen	(14)	15	19	17
ghteen	8	11	(18)	14
rteen	14	12	(13)	19
neteen	12	9	(19)	17

Page 153

12, 11
13, 14

Page 154

16, 17
15, 18

Page 166

4, 5, 6, 7, 8, 9
11, 12, 13, 14, 15

Page 167

Page 168

Page 169

Page 170

2, 1
3, 2

Page 171

4
4
6
5

Page 172

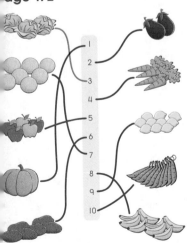

Page 173

 2

 4

 6

Page 174

4, 1
3, 5
6, 10
2, 8
7, 9

Page 175

4, 9
6, 3
7, 10
5, 8

Pages 176–177

 8   4

 5   7

6   1

Pages 178–179

 2   2

4   7

 8   4

 6   3

Page 180

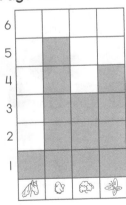

6			
5			
4			
3			
2			
1			

Answer Key

Page 181

Pages 182-183

5   3

3   2

7   5

Pages 184-185

Animals with 2 legs						
Animals with 4 legs						
	1	2	3	4	5	6

Pages 186-187

4   12

6   10

9   7

Pages 188-189

6   10

2   8

5   12

Pages 190-191

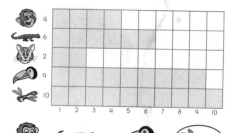

Page 193

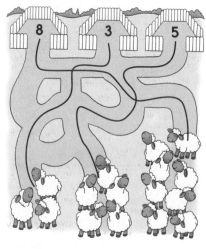

8   3   5

Page 194

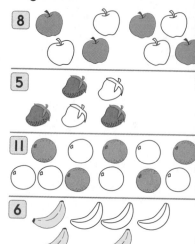

8

5

11

6

Page 195

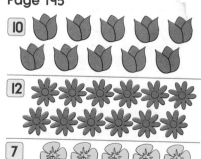

10

12

7

9

Page 196

3
6
1
2

Page 197

1   4
3   8
9   5
2   7
6   10

Page 198

4   3
7   6
5   9
8   2

Page 199

2   7
11   8
6   4
9   10
5   7

Page 200

7
10
4
6

Page 201

7   3
10   6
4   8
11   5
9   12

Page 202

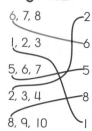

6, 7, 8   2
1, 2, 3   6
5, 6, 7   5
2, 3, 4   8
8, 9, 10   1

Page 203

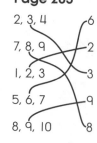

2, 3, 4   6
7, 8, 9   2
1, 2, 3   3
5, 6, 7   9
8, 9, 10   8